The Big
Book of BUDS 2

The Big Book of BUDS

volume 2

More Marijuana
Varieties from the
World's Great
Seed Breeders

Quick American Archives

The Big Book of Buds Volume 2
1st edition, 2nd printing
Copyright 2004 Quick American

Photographs in The Big Book of Buds Volume 2
appear courtesy of the contributors, who each retain copyright to their work.

Published by Quick American
A division of Quick Trading Company
Oakland, California
0-932551-62-9

Managing Editor: S. Newhart
Editor: Ed Rosenthal
Sponsorship Coordinator: Jaloola
Cover and Interior Design: Scott Idleman/Blink
Cover photo: Flying Dutchmen's Thai-Tanic, photo courtesy Cannabis College
Printed in China.

Variety descriptions and breeder stories compiled by S. Newhart with the assistance of John Carnahan.

We wish to thank all Big Book of Buds 2 contributors for providing articles, information and photos. Without your participation and support, this project would not have been possible.

Publisher's Cataloging-in-Publication
(Provided by Quality Books)

Rosenthal, Ed.
    The big book of buds. Volume 2, More marijuana
varieties from the world's great seed breeders / Ed
Rosenthal.
    p. cm.
    Includes index

    1. Marijuana. 2. Cannabis. I. Title.

SB295.C35R67 2004   633.79
                QBI04-800012

This book is dedicated to François Rabelais and to Pantagruel, the inventors of Pantagruelion.

See that girl, barefootin' along,
whistling and singing, she's a carrying on.
There's laughing in her eyes,
dancing in her feet,
she's a neon light diamond and she can
live on the street.

From "The Golden Road (to Unlimited Devotion)"
Lyrics and music by McGannahan Skjellyfetti
Copyright Ice Nine Publishing
Courtesy the Grateful Dead

Contents

Introduction

Introduction

By Ed Rosenthal

Researchers think that cannabis originated in the Himalayan foothills. The climate there is temperate and the weather changes from year to year. To survive in such an environment, annual plants retain some individuality. Genetically speaking, plants accomplish this by keeping diverse genes within a single group of plants. That way, some do better in wet years; others are more successful during heat waves or drought or overcast skies.

This heterogeneity came in handy when humans carried cannabis to new lands with different climates. The emigrant plants had genes tucked away, preparing them to adapt to new conditions. Cannabis traveled far and wide, first along the caravan routes that crossed to China, India and the Mid-East. It is believed they then made it around the Mediterranean and into Africa, and finally to the smaller island countries. When the first European ships cruised to the Americas they brought cannabis for the ride and it adapted well there, too.

For millennia, civilizations found industrial uses for cannabis. Its fiber was valued for strength, durability and versatility. The Vedic, Chinese and Mid-Eastern cultures found recreational and therapeutic uses as well. When north European cultures "discovered" marijuana's effects, the stage was set for a collision between the herb and the societal ethics.

The non-linear thought processes of marijuana intoxication were probably not the reason for pothibition, but it was the rationale trotted out to the public. Marijuana's foreignness and its association with minorities and disreputable entertainers made it an easy target.

In the book, *The Botany of Desire,* Michael Pollan noted that pothibition has been a boon to the species marijuana. He showed that restrictive laws forced the development of technology to grow it in a vast new environment: indoors under lights. Pothibition created a domestic supply network that made its cultivation more popular than ever.

The laws have made it difficult for people to obtain seed or young plants as they would if they were growing tomatoes. Thus government policies have inadvertently promoted a breeding program exceeded by no commercial plant. Tens of thousands of gardeners have played roles in developing varieties by selecting from their best. Occasionally a single plant or a small group of plants shows outstanding qualities that bring it fame and sometimes fortune.

From the beginning of breeding using the classic landraces to the cosmopolitan varieties available today, only forty years has passed. Over those years, plants have progressed through many generations, with each better adapted to its new homeland, or to growing indoors under a strict regime of lights. Breeders have played a role in improving plants over generations, constantly selecting plants that were higher in potency and easier to grow.

The first book in this series, *The Big Book of Buds,* was testimony to the work of breeders who developed many of the newly re-domesticated varieties. They proved that cannabis' variability could be manipulated to make it a plant that could be grown by the home gardener. Many of these strains became legendary and have been relied on as parent stock in successive breeding endeavors.

Cannabis is enjoying the new territories it has colonized indoors and out, and continues to evolve in its symbiotic relationship with humans. The anti-drug ads are right (well at least in one way): today's marijuana is not the same as your parents or grandparents. It's more user-friendly and much easier to grow.

Big Book of Buds Volume 2 is a celebration of the two-fold path taken by seed breeders since the *Big Book of Buds* was published. First, they have developed plants that are more adapted to specific conditions. Plants may grow tall and branchy, short and bonsai-like, or be limber enough to grow like a vine. Some are tolerant of cold, heat, drought, short or long seasons and so many other important factors.

Second, breeders have more specifically elucidated marijuana's effects on humans. All pot isn't the same. Some takes you up, some takes you down and still others take you all kinds of side ways. As we have more scientific research about this plant and its components, the medicinal, mental and physiological effects of each variety can cater more to a specifically desired effect.

The Big Book of Buds Volume 2 opens a new chapter in the evolution of our relationship to this plant. Marijuana and humans go back millennia but this book is about the modern cannabis plant, as gardeners adapt it to fit our contemporary needs, desires and circumstances.

May the two species continue to dance together.

The Icons

The first icon deals with plant type. The possibilities are:

S   plants with a sativa background

I   plants with an indica background

and hybrids, which are either

SI   more sativa

IS   more indica

I   Indica plants originated around the 30th parallel in the Hindu Kush region of the Himalayan foothills. This includes the countries of Afghanistan, Pakistan, Tajikistan, Northern India and Nepal. The weather there is quite variable from year to year. For this reason the populations there have a varied gene pool and even within a particular population there is a high degree of heterogeneity, which results in plants of the same variety having quite a bit of variability. This helps the population survive. No matter what the weather during a particular year, some plants will thrive and reproduce.

These plants are fairly short, usually under 5 feet tall. They are bushy with compact branching and short internodes. They range in shape from a rounded bush to a pine-like shape with a wide base. The leaves are short, very wide and a darker shade of green than most equatorial sativas because they contain larger amounts of chlorophyll. Sometimes there is webbing between the leaflets. At the 30th latitude, the plants don't receive as much light as plants at or near the equator. By increasing the amount of chlorophyll, the cells use light more efficiently.

Indica buds are dense and tight. They form several shapes depending on variety. All of them are chunky or blocky. Sometimes they form continuous clusters along the stem. They have intense smells ranging from acrid, skunky, or musky to equally pungent aromas. Indica smoke is dense, lung expanding and cough inducing. The high is heavy, body-oriented and lethargic.

S   Sativa plants grow from the equator through the 50th parallel. They include both marijuana and hemp varieties. The plants that marijuana growers are interested in come from the equator to the 20th parallel. Countries from this area are noted for high-grade marijuana and include Colombia, Jamaica, Nigeria, Congo, Thailand and Sumatra. Populations of plants from most of these areas are quite uniform for several reasons. Cannabis is not native to these areas. It was imported to grow hemp crops and then it adapted over many generations with human intervention. Each population originated from a small amount of fairly uniform seed from the 45-50th parallel. Then the populations evolved over hundreds of generations with the help of humans. This led to fairly uniform populations in climates that varied little year to year.

Sativas grow into 5-15 feet tall symmetrical pine-shaped plants. The spaces between the leaves on the stem, the internodes, are longer on sativas than indicas. This helps to give sativas a taller stature. The lowest branches are the widest, spreading 1 to 3 feet; since the branches grow opposite each other, plant diameter may reach 6 feet. The leaves are long, slender and finger-like. The plants are light green since they contain less chlorophyll.

Sativa buds are lighter than indicas. Some varieties grow buds along the entire branch, developing a thin but dense cola. Others grow large formations of very light buds. The smoke is sweet, spicy or fruity. The highs are described as soaring, psychedelic, thoughtful and spacy.

IS Indica-sativa hybrids naturally tend towards the indica side of the family. They usually have controlled height. They don't grow very tall and after forcing flowering, their growth is limited. Their side branching is usually not prominent and they can be grown in a small space.

SI Sativa-indica hybrids tend towards the sativa parentage. They are taller plants, which will grow to double or triple their size if they are forced when they are small. They are usually hard to grow in a sea of green, as the plants demand more space to spread out.

With the many combinations and complex parentages of modern hybrids, it is impossible to generalize about the qualities of hybrids' smoke, highs or other characteristics. So many plants have been crossed and their progeny used for breeding that it is truly a mixed-up world out there.

The second icon details the number of days it takes the plant to ripen after forcing flowering. Both environmental conditions and subjective factors affect maturation.

Take, for instance, one experiment in which identical plants grown indoors in a lab were fed different water-soluble commercial fertilizers. These identical plants grown with identical conditions save the fertilizers ripened up to 10 days apart. The fertilizers also affected the taste and quality of the buds.

Plant growth and maturation is also affected by temperature. Both cold and hot conditions interfere with ripening. Temperate conditions encourage fast growth and prompt ripening.

The planting method is another factor that affects ripening time. Hydroponic plants mature earlier than their sisters in planting medium.

I would call a plant ripe when the "resin" in the glands starts to turn milky or amber. This is about a week later than some people prefer. The taste differs and the cannabinoids may change a bit, resulting in different highs. Dutch coffeeshops often sell bud that is immature. The glands are there, but have not filled completely with THC. The high is racing and buzzy. I don't find it that satisfying. Obviously, ripening time is affected by your idea of ripeness.

It is easy to see that the numbers mentioned are intended to give the reader an approximation rather than hard figures. While they offer an indication of what you should expect, they shouldn't be used to figure your timetable.

Plants that are recommended for growing outdoors indicate the maturity date under natural light. When no latitude is mentioned, figure the month indicated is at the same latitude as the country of origin. For Holland, the latitude is 52 degrees. Canadian seeds are produced at the 50 degrees latitude and Spanish seeds are produced at the 40-41 degrees latitude.

The third icon indicates recommendations for planting. The choices are:

 indoor   outdoor, or

 indoor/outdoor

Outdoor strains may do well in a greenhouse setup, but will be difficult to grow indoors. They may require too much light for inside growing, and usually have their own ideas about growth and height, making them hard to tame. The problem with most plants not recommended for outdoors in temperate climates is that the plants don't ripen by the end of the season. Some plants rated as indoor plants can be grown outdoors if they are forced to flower early using shade cloth. As an example, a plant which ripens in mid-November, 45 days after a gardener's September 30th harvest schedule, could be coaxed to flower early by covering it with opaque plastic each evening at 6 pm and removing it at 6 am the next morning beginning July 1, through late-August. Most varieties will ripen within 90 days.

The fourth icon is a report of expected yield. These figures are somewhat ambiguous since the results are not reported consistently. Cannabis, as all green plants, uses light to fuel photosynthesis. The sugars produced become tissue. As a shortcut, you could say Light=Growth. Yields vary first and foremost due to light conditions, so space or plant definitions are incomplete by themselves. The yields that appear here assume that indoor gardens are receiving at least 600 watts per meter (wpm) where no light wattage is indicated.

The fifth icon is listed only on plants suitable for **sea of green** gardens. Plants in these gardens are spaced together very closely so that each plant needs to grow little if any to fill the canopy. Plants are forced to flower soon after they are placed in the flowering space. Eliminating the vegetative growth stage decreases turnaround. SOG gardens hold 3 to 6 plants per square foot.

The sixth icon is the parentage of the variety. While this can get quite complex, you get an idea of what the possibilities are for any variety by knowing its parents.

Some of the hybrids in the book are f2 unstabilized. When pure strains (let's call them strains A & B) are crossed and a hybrid is produced, the first generation, the f1 hybrid plants, are all uniform because they all contain the same genes. One set from the female and one set from the male. When two f1's are crossed, the seeds receive a random assortment of genes. For each of the more than 100,000 sets of genes, a plant may get two genes from A, one each from A and B, or two from B. No two plants are alike.

To stabilize them so that they have similar characteristics, the plants are inbred for five or six generations creating an F6, using careful selections. However breeders often work with unstabilized hybrids, which has an advantage when breeding for cloning.

Stability can be judged in part by the number of parents a variety has. Pure strains are the most uniform, since they are not recombining different genetic dispositions. Hybrids have the advantage of gaining vigor from the fresh combination. They also vary more. Strains with three or four parents are likely to exhibit more than one phenotype when grown out. When the three parents are hybrids themselves, the combination can result in quite a bit of diversity.

Diversity is not bad. Consider a gardener starting out. Clones are taken once the plants grow some side stems. When the plants have been harvested and tasted the gardener decides to select two plants for the next garden. Clones of those plants are grown vegetatively and used for mothers. If the seed line was uniform as it is with pure strains or stabilized varieties, there would not be much difference between the plants. Seeds from an unstabilized variety give the gardener more choices.

The seventh icon is the one that is most important to me. What is the buzz like? Describing a state of mind is not an easy task. Separating one's mind state from the state of mind created by the brain's interplay with cannabinoids is subtle. We have used many terms to describe this state: active • alert • blissful • body relaxation • calm • cheerful • clear • couchlock • creeper • dreamy • electric • energetic • euphoric • even head/body high • eyedroop • functional • giddy • giggly • happy • hazy • heady • intense • lethargic • longlasting • lucid • mellow • mind numbing • munchies • narcotic • physical • playful • positive • psychedelic • sedative • sensual • soaring • social • stoney • talkative • thoughtful • trippy • uplifting • wandering mind

The eighth icon, the final one, is a short, 1-3 word description of the smell and taste. The odors we included are: acrid • berry • bubblegum • candy • caramel • chocolate • cinnamon • citrus • coffee • dark • earthy • floral • fresh • fruity • fuel • grapefruit • hash • haze • herbal • honey • lavender • lemon • licorice • mango • melon • metal • mild • minty • musky • nutty • orange • pepper • pine • pineapple • pungent • sage • sandalwood • sour • spicy • strawberry • sweet • tart • Thai stick • tobacco • tropical • whiskey • wildflower • woodsy

Once again, fuller descriptions are found in the text.

The icons are fast reference points. They give you an idea of where the story is going. The accompanying variety description fleshes out this information with more nuanced details and tips about the plant's preferences. Every story offers something a little different. Together, they offer an intersting look at marijuana breeding today. Enjoy!

Quick Key to Icons

English • En Español • Deutsch
En Français • Italiano • Dutch

Strain Type

Sativa

Indica

Sativa/Indica

Indica/Sativa

Growing Info

Flowering time
Tiempo de floración
Blütezeit
Durée de floraison
Stagione della fioritura
Bloetijd

Parents
Genética
Mutterpflanze
Descendance
Genitori
Stamboom

Yield
Rendimiento
Ertag
Rendement
Raccolta
Opbrengst

Indoor
Interior
Drinnen
d'Intérieur
Dentro
Binnen

Outdoor
Exterior
Draussen
d'Extérieur
Fuori
Buiten

Indoor/Outdoor
Interior/Exterior
Drinnen/Draussen
d'Intérieur/d'Extérieur
Dentro/Fuori
Binnen/Buiten

Sea of Green

Sensory Experience

Buzz
Efecto
die Art des Turns
Effets
Effetti
High Effekt

Taste/Smell
Sabor/Aroma
Geschmack/Geruch
Saveur/Arôme
Sapore/Odore
Smaak/Geua

Breeder Location

South Africa

Australia

Canada

Netherlands

Spain

Afghanica • Ambrosia • Aurora Indica • Australian Blue • Baby Be...
Brains Escape • Bronze Whaler • California Grapefruit • Candy Cane Brain • C
Diamond Head • Double Dutch • Dreadlock • Ducksfoot • Dutch Treat x North
Euforia • Exile • G13-Haze x NYC Diesel • God's Treat • Hawaiian Snow • He
Kerala Krush • Lethal Purple • Lionheart • Lowryder • Magic Bud • Manitoba P
-Ultra • Moroc x Afgan • New York City Diesel • Nirvana Special • Orange Bud
Treat • Rocklock • RockStar • Rox • Sage 'n Sour • Sapphire Star • Sativa Spir
• Sour Diesel • StarGazer • Strawberry Cough • Sugar Babe • Super Shit • Sw
Light • White Star • Afghanica • Ambrosia • Aurora Indica • Australian Blue • B
• Brains Damage • Brains Escape • Bronze Whaler • California Grapefruit • Ca
• Danky Doodle • Diamond Head • Double Dutch • Dreadlock • Ducksfoot • I
Ethiopian Highland • Euforia • Exile • G13-Haze x NYC Diesel • God's Treat • H
#39 • KC #42 • Kerala Krush • Lethal Purple • Lionheart • Lowryder • Magic Bu
• Mikush • MK-Ultra • Moroc x Afgan • New York City Diesel • Nirvana Special
Skunk x Dutch Treat • Rocklock • RockStar • Rox • Sage 'n Sour • Sapphire St
Amnesia Haze • Sour Diesel • StarGazer • Strawberry Cough • Sugar Babe •
Warlock • White Light • White Star • Afghanica • Ambrosia • Aurora Indica • Au
• Brains Choice • Brains Damage • Brains Escape • Bronze Whaler • California
• Cinderella 99 • Danky Doodle • Diamond Head • Double Dutch • Dreadlock
Endless Sky • Ethiopian Highland • Euforia • Exile • G13-Haze x NYC Diesel • (
Surprise • KC #39 • KC #42 • Kerala Krush • Lethal Purple • Lionheart • Lowry
Mint • Mazar • Mikush • MK-Ultra • Moroc x Afgan • New York City Diesel • N
Plant • Purple Skunk x Dutch Treat • Rocklock • RockStar • Rox • Sage 'n Sou
White • Soma's Amnesia Haze • Sour Diesel • StarGazer • Strawberry Cough
Green • Waldo • Warlock • White Light • White Star • Afghanica • Ambrosia • Au
• Bluberry Haze • Brains Choice • Brains Damage • Brains Escape • Bronze W
Cherry Pez Livity • Cinderella 99 • Danky Doodle • Diamond Head • Double D
Swazi Skunk • Endless Sky • Ethiopian Highland • Euforia • Exile • G13-Haz

BUDS

Blue Pearl • Bluberry Haze • Brains Choice • Brains Damage
...lope Haze • CannaSutra • Cherry Pez Livity • Cinderella 99 • Danky Doodle
...Lights • Early Sativa • Early Swazi Skunk • Endless Sky • Ethiopian Highland
...Duty Fruity • Jack Flash • Kalichakra • Kariba Surprise • KC #39 • KC #42 •
...• Maple Leaf Indica • Marley's Collie • Matanuska Mint • Mazar • Mikush • MK
...paya • Passion Queen • Pineapple Punch • Power Plant • Purple Skunk x Dutch
...Satori • Shiesel • Shiva • Skydog • Slyder • Snow White • Soma's Amnesia Haze
...Bliss • Tanzanian Magic • Thai-Tanic • Transkei Green • Waldo • Warlock • White
...Early • Blue God • Blue Grape #1 • Blue Pearl • Bluberry Haze • Brains Choice
...Cane Brain • Cannalope Haze • CannaSutra • Cherry Pez Livity • Cinderella 99
...h Treat x Northern Lights • Early Sativa • Early Swazi Skunk • Endless Sky •
...ian Snow • He...y...ruity...arly...Surprise • KC
...Manitoba Pois...ala...eaf...arle...Cy...Ma...us...int • Mazar
...ange Bud • Pa...sio...ee...nc...ne...e...-...Plant • Purple
...Sativa Spirit •...ese...hi...k...ite • Soma's
...r Shit • Swiss...h...su...y...a • Waldo •
...an Blue • Bid...Cherry Haze
...efruit • Candy...Ha...Sutra...Pez Livity
...cksfoot • Dutch Treat x Northern Lights • Early Sativa • Early Swazi Skunk •
...Treat • Hawaiian Snow • Heavy Duty Fruity • Jack Flash • Kalichakra • Kariba
...Magic Bud • Manitoba Poison • Maple Leaf Indica • Marley's Collie • Matanuska
...a Special • Orange Bud • Papaya • Passion Queen • Pineapple Punch • Power
...apphire Star • Sativa Spirit • Satori • Shiesel • Shiva • Skydog • Slyder • Snow
...gar Babe • Super Shit • Swiss Bliss • Tanzanian Magic • Thai-Tanic • Transke
...Indica • Australian Blue • Biddy Early • Blue God • Blue Grape #1 • Blue Pear
...• California Grapefruit • Candy Cane Brain • Cannalope Haze • CannaSutra •
...• Dreadlock • Ducksfoot • Dutch Treat x Northern Lights • Early Sativa • Early
...YC Diesel • God's Treat • Hawaiian Snow • Heavy Duty Fruity • Jack Flash

Photo: Cannabis College

Afghanica

Flying Dutchmen

 62.5/37.5

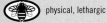 physical, lethargic

 acrid, pungent

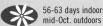 56-63 days indoors
mid-Oct. outdoors

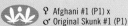 ♀ Afghani #1 (P1) x
♂ Original Skunk #1 (P1)

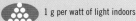 1 g per watt of light indoors

Afghanica is an F1 hybrid that is true to its roots. This predominantly indica plant grows short and stocky, with broad leaves and a thick canopy. Afghanica produces well when gardened inside or outdoors in most temperate regions, but yields are heaviest when it is grown in a sea of green (12-16 plants psm or 3-4 plants psf). Trim away lower branches before the onset of flowering; this allows the plant to devote all available energy to the light-immersed tops. Removing lower branches outdoors late in the season also increases airflow, limiting potential mold or pest problems.

In a normal season, Afghanica matures into a 6-foot (2-meter) tall Christmas tree, and may exhibit red or purple coloration in colder climates. No matter where she is grown, organic soil will foster a sweeter, more refined end product. Afghanica has low-to-medium nutrient requirements. Too many nutrients in the latter stages of maturation impair the taste. No nutrients should be given for the last 10 days before harvest. Although this strain often looks ready well before its 8-9 weeks of flowering are finished, the yield and potency increase tremendously in the last week. It is worth the wait.

When nearing harvest, Afghanica plants emit a petrol-type aroma at the slightest disturbance. The buds are fairly dense and very oily throughout. The coated smaller leaves are worth collecting, as they produce an abundance of heavy, oily resin when put through a screen. Smell and taste are typical Afghani—acrid, pungent and volatile, although the Skunk father lends a little sweetness. The high is potent, lethargic and physical in nature. It comes on slowly and has a longlasting depth and density. If smoked late at night the effects can often still be felt in the morning. Medicinally, Afghanica is effective relief for insomnia and chronic pain.

Ambrosia

Jordan of the Islands

In Greek and Roman mythology, Ambrosia is the name given to the food of the gods. Perhaps this plant complements the menu with a smoke worthy of this term's general definition: "something sweetly pleasing in taste or smell." The Burmese sativa mother of this plant came from Mighty Mite Seed Company, and was voted the #1 People's Choice in the 2002 *Cannabis Culture* Toker's Bowl. The father, Jordan's God Bud strain, is a mostly indica plant that gained popularity because of its powerful, desirable aroma and a flavor leaning toward tropical sweetness.

Ambrosia grows well in a sea of green using hydro or soil methods. Outdoors this plant does best in locales with long days during the summer. Its growth habits meld together aspects from both sides of the family tree, resulting in a plant that reaches a happy medium in height, foliage and coloration. Ambrosia is a fast, vigorous grower. She will become bushy if there is room, but tends to not be very leafy, which makes manicuring a little less painstaking. With average fertilizer use and good garden conditions, Ambrosia produces a respectable yield of buds that are dense, sticky and redolent of classic mellow dank skunkiness. The leaves yellow and the hairs turn strongly orange to clearly indicate ripe readiness.

Ambrosia's smoke is appropriately sweet and complex, with just enough skunk to keep it traditional. The Ambrosia buzz stays on the sativa end of the spectrum, producing an awake, up high that comes on fast and stays functional. This makes Ambrosia a good all-day smoke.

 50/50

 alert, active

 sweet & skunky

 50-56 days indoors
mid-Sept. outdoors

 ♀ Burmese x ♂ God Bud

 4-8 oz. per plant indoors
8-12 oz. per plant outdoors

Aurora Indica

Nirvana

Imagine yourself looking out on a clear dark night high in the Northern hemisphere. A faint greenish glow forms a lazy arch across the sky. It ripples like a giant cosmic curtain, and as if by magic, warm hues of red and purple emerge through the green, filling the sky as if scattered by a big puff of wind, then slowly fading back to a simple and subtle green sea of light. This is the aurora, also the name of the Greek goddess whose dance precedes the dawn—and of Nirvana's potent, hashy cross of its Northern Lights and Afghan strains.

This F1 hybrid has all the characteristics of a strong indica: the branching stays low and close with strong, thick stems. Its compact, sturdy structure favors the sea of green method, placed in flowering at 18 inches (50 cm) and ripe at under 3 feet (1 meter), but keep an eye out for mold if your environment warrants it. The pistils stay white upon ripening, but in cold environments the leaves may turn red. Don't wait for all the hairs to turn before harvesting.

Aurora Indica's leaves are dark and impressively wide and its smell is dense and spicy, leading gardeners to anticipate the cosmic indica experience its name suggests. The buds are thick and greasy to the touch, with a deep Afghani flavor that is more apparent when grown in soil. A great stone before bed, this heavy buzz comes on quick and can be quite sedative. People have reported hot ears as a common side effect when vaporizing. This strain has medicinal potential for treating hyperactivity and insomnia.

 90/10

 sedative

 spicy

 55-60 days hydro
60-65 days soil

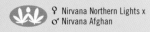 ♀ Nirvana Northern Lights x
♂ Nirvana Afghan

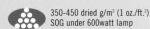 350-450 dried g/m² (1 oz./ft.²)
SOG under 600watt lamp

 SOG

Australian Blue

Homegrown Fantaseeds

Photo: Marco

Australian Blue crosses Homegrown Fantaseed's prizewinning strain, Blue Haze, with an Australian sativa given to them in 1999 by some friends from down under. Australia is well known as one of the great global spots for sativas. Blue's 90% sativa mother, the "Duck" or "Boesi" strain, contributes a classic sativa high and the clean musk of a lemon grove to this hybrid.

The haze influence combined with the dominant sativa make Australian Blue a leggy plant that loves to branch and get tall. She forms branches from the bottom and grows into a slender Christmas-tree shape. You don't have to be in Australia to get good results with Australian Blue, but you do need to be in a locale where the weather supports an 11-week flowering cycle and the thermometer stays above 17° Celsius (62° Fahrenheit). In locations that don't meet these criteria, Australian Blue can be grown indoors. Homegrown Fantaseeds prefers gardening this variety in soil. Indoors, the average expected yield is ¾ ounce (20-25 grams) per plant, a fairly typical sativa yield.

The buzz from a haze-sativa is lucid and uplifting, sometimes bordering on the psychedelic. When harvested too early, it can be a little speedy, but at the proper maturation, Australian Blue delivers the type of high sativa fans love—thoughtful and euphoric, relaxed yet awake and ready to enjoy what the day sends you.

 90/10

 lucid, uplifting

 lemon

 75-80 days

 ♀ Australian Duck x ♂ Blue Haze

 20-25 g (¾ oz.) per plant

Biddy Early
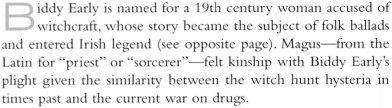

Magus Genetics

 50/50

 stoney, dizzying

 sweet, candy

 50 to 60 days indoors
end Sept/ beg. Oct. outdoor

 Early Skunk (F2) x Warlock

 300-400 g/m² (1-1¹/₃ oz./ft.²)
indoors
Approx. 300 g (10 oz.) per
plant outdoors

Biddy Early is named for a 19th century woman accused of witchcraft, whose story became the subject of folk ballads and entered Irish legend (see opposite page). Magus—from the Latin for "priest" or "sorcerer"—felt kinship with Biddy Early's plight given the similarity between the witch hunt hysteria in times past and the current war on drugs.

Biddy Early is the first variety that Magus Genetics specifically formulated for outdoor gardening in temperate regions. Although an even mix of sativa and indica, this plant exhibits the strong lateral growth typically seen in sativas. Biddy likes to branch out. The branches are very elastic and pliable, easily trained or tied like vines to suit the available space. Outdoors, this suppleness makes the plant "storm proof" or resilient to harsh weather.

Biddy Early shows her talents outdoors, but may create trouble when grown indoors either for bud or as mothers for cloning, due to her low flowering trigger. Biddy often flowers prematurely if stressed by a lack of sufficient light, nutrients, or root space.

At maturity, Biddy Early is a medium-sized plant that delivers a respectable yield of sugary sweet colas. The buzz mixes sativa headiness and indica power for a somewhat unbalancing broomstick ride into an enjoyably floaty high. Warm ears are a common side effect.

The Biddy Early plant has gained renown in Europe and beyond, winning multiple awards in recent years—the Silver (sativa category) at the *High Times* Cannabis Cup in 2003, and second place (outdoor category) at the Highlife Cup in 2004.

Struck by the similarity between the war on drugs and the witch hunts of times past, Magus Genetics named its Biddy Early strain for a legendary "witch" of County Clare, Ireland.

In the 19th century, County Clare was one of Ireland's poorest districts. Its Gaelic peasants suffered the full weight of famine, evictions, emigration and punitive laws forbidding the native Irish language and Catholic faith. For religion, cultural lore and medicine, peasants turned to "hedge doctors"—social outsiders who offered a mixture of folk medicine and superstition.

Brighid "Biddy" O'Conner, known by her mother's maiden name "Early," was orphaned and evicted from her family home in 1814 at the age of sixteen. She wandered Western Ireland as an itinerant laborer at one point working for a physician, who may have taught her some conventional medicine – before settling in the village of Feakle. There, she lived with a series of husbands and lovers and worked as a hedge doctor or wise woman, telling fortunes and curing ailments in return for food and whiskey.

Countless legends and ballads celebrate Biddy Early's generosity to travelers, her ageless allure to men, and the magic she could work with the blue bottle she always carried, said to contain the spirit of her dead son, Tom. Biddy's alleged powers included the ability to stop sheriffs from carrying out evictions; perhaps because of this, the Anglo-Irish authorities tried her under a medieval witchcraft law in 1865, but she was acquitted because nobody from Feakle would testify against her. Biddy Early died in 1874. Her name lives on in pubs and tourist landmarks, and in the writings of literary giants like Augusta Gregory and W.B. Yeats, both of whom collected stories about Biddy from the villagers of Feakle.

Photo: Green Born Identity

Starting Seeds Right

By Ed Rosenthal

Seeds are the distillation of a plant's essence. They contain the blueprint for life, which they hold in storage until they sense environmental conditions that favor survival of a new plant.

Once they've made contact with the requisite amount of moisture and proper range of warmth, seeds start the process of germination. A cascade of chemical reactions results in the rapid growth of the embryo plant, which has been kept in suspended animation.

Marijuana seeds germinate best at room temperature, around 72° F, in a consistently moist environment. The first visible sign that a seed is in germination mode is that it increases in size slightly as it absorbs water. Then a small opening appears along the seed's seam as the root emerges. The root continues to elongate as the stem makes its appearance. It stretches out in the opposite direction of the root and uncurls, revealing two embryonic leaves called cotyledons. The seed case is now an empty shell and its remnants may hang onto one of the cotyledons until blown or rubbed off. Only a day or so elapses between the first sight of the root and the appearance of the first set of seedling leaves.

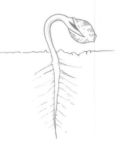

Once the root has appeared, germination is complete. In its first phase of growth, the seedling used energy stored in the seed for fuel, but now it must produce its own food as its roots seek moisture and nutrients. It does this through photosynthesis. The root grows longer and extends branches while the first set of true leaves emerge at the tip or apex of the stem, which is called the apical tip.

Healthy germination is an auspicious start for a successful plant. Again, when the plant's needs are met, the seedling will grow and prosper. Growers use different methods of germinating seed.

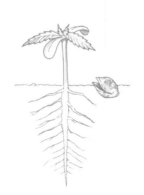

One germination method:

The seeds are soaked in a solution of water with commercial rooting solution and hydrogen peroxide for 12 hours. The hormones in the rooting solution stimulate germination and encourage root growth. Rooting solution is used as per instructions for softwood cuttings and the hydrogen peroxide is added at the rate of one part to 200, (½ %) to sterilize the solution, preventing infection. Drugstore peroxide is a 3% solution, so it's added at the rate of one part H_2O_2 to five parts water.

After soaking, seeds are placed in the rooting material that they are to grow in. In planting mix, they are placed ½-inch deep in sterile commercial planting mix. Each seed is placed in its own 2-inch square container. The mix is moistened with water adjusted to a pH of around 6.2-6.5, and then kept in a bright space with high moisture. If the space is dry, a piece of plastic wrap can be placed loosely over the containers to reduce evaporation. The containers are kept at room temperature. If the air is cool, an electrical tray warmer can be used.

If the plants are to be grown aeroponically or hydroponically, they are placed in the medium in which they'll be grown. Oasis® or rockwool cubes can be used to grow out the seedlings if that is inconvenient. Both of these mediums are sterile. Oasis cubes need no preparation. Rockwool cubes have an alkaline pH that affects plants. To buffer them, the rockwool is first soaked in water with an

Photo: Ed Borg

acidic pH of about 5.8 for a day. Then they can be used just like the Oasis cubes. First, the tray of cubes is dipped in water with a pH between 6 and 6.5. Again the seeds are placed ½-inch deep. The planted tray should be kept in a brightly lit area at room temperature, and the cubes should always be kept moist without being water-logged.

Another germination method:

Seeds are placed between moist cloths or towels in a covered dish. The dish is kept at room temperature and checked several times a day for signs of germination. At the first indication of growth, the seed is transferred to planting medium.

As soon as the seedlings appear they are fertilized with a weak solution of a flowering formula fertilizer. The high phosphorous in these flowering-specific fertilizers encourages vigorous root growth. After the appearance of the first true leaves, the fertilizer is changed to a vegetative growth formula, which is used as directed.

The main problem that people encounter when germinating is stretchy seedlings. This is an indication of insufficient light intensity. To encourage strong, stout stems that don't stretch, seedlings must be provided with intense light from the start—a minimum of 40-60 watts per square foot (400-600 watts per square meter). When handled properly, quality seeds should be sprouting in no time.

10

Bluberry Haze

DNA Genetics

Photos: Donja

Bluberry Haze prefers some pampering, but when given proper love and attention, she delivers a high that will turn heads.

Hazes have increased in popularity over the last few years, especially in breeding programs. They are especially suitable for crossing. The pure Haze, an equatorial, offers an exciting taste and high, but can be too much trouble for the average home grower. Hazes are long season plants that grow very tall and lanky, demanding space and patience without the high yields that other plants provide under similar conditions. Once crossed with shorter season plants, the Haze's flowering time and size may both be brought back into a range that is reasonable for the average gardener. Bluberry Haze crosses a secret haze with the signature DJ Short Blueberry, a more compact plant with purple-blue foliage, a berry-flavor to the smoke, and a popular high. The result is a 9-10 week flowering period. This hybrid likes to branch and darkens to a forest green late in flowering. The buds are nice-formed tight nuggets.

Still, Bluberry Haze is a plant for people who like to garden, not for home or commercial growers seeking an easy crop. She can be persnickety and will show her displeasure if the garden is not kept clean and well regulated within favorable light and temperature conditions. But smoke connoisseurs are likely to find Bluberry Haze worth the effort. This hybrid inherits the taste that goes with the name: a succulent berry flavor with a bit of the fresh herbal hue of the Haze. The true reward is the quality of the high, which builds from a mild feeling of wellness to euphoria, inspiration, and a perma-grin. The potency and gradual onset require some experience and pacing; overuse may turn an enjoyable buzz into sweet dreams as overwhelming drowsiness kicks in.

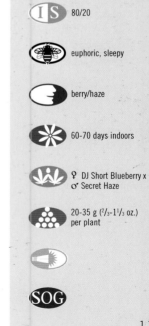

IS 80/20

euphoric, sleepy

berry/haze

60-70 days indoors

♀ DJ Short Blueberry x ♂ Secret Haze

20-35 g (²/₃-1¹/₃ oz.) per plant

SOG

11

Blue God

Jordan of the Islands

Blue God, the clever name given to the offspring of God Bud and Blueberry, evokes the Hindu deity Krishna—eighth avatar of Vishnu, Bhagavad Gita teacher, master of internal yogas and upholder of the cosmic order. Scholars and priests debate the connotations of Krishna's blue-black skin. It can suggest the profound and peaceful expanse of the sky and sea, and a power distinct from the other gods and heroes. For Jordan's Blue God strain, blue pigment mainly shows its enviable Blueberry parentage.

Blue God does well indoors or can grow outside in areas with a long season. It is best to grow the short, dense and bushy Blue God as a multi-branch plant. Jordan prefers gardening this strain in soil over the hydro method. Indoors, Blue God reaches 3-4 feet in height and gets just as wide at the base. Outside, this solid indica can reach 8-12 feet, crowded with massive buds and thick leaves that turn dark purple as it matures.

Even though Blue God will show incredible resin at 6-7 weeks, wise growers let it go 8 weeks for maximum yields. Blue God gives a very strong indica nightcap high. Sleep and relief from chronic pain can come on fast; the strain doesn't suit activities that require alertness and energy. The smoke tastes somewhat the way the plant looks, deep with a hint of berry. Blue God won 4th place in the *Cannabis Culture* Toker's Bowl 2002.

I

sleepy/lethargic

berry

55-60 days

♀ God Bud x ♂ Blueberry

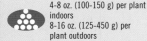
4-8 oz. (100-150 g) per plant indoors
8-16 oz. (125-450 g) per plant outdoors

Blue Grape #1

Electric Seed Co.

Blue Grape #1 is a hybrid favoring the indica side of the spectrum yet offering a somewhat sativa-like high. Electric Seed Company originated this strain by pollinating a stout bushy Grapefruit female with a Blueberry male chosen for its vigorous growth and hardiness. The Grapefruit and Blueberry strains were developed in North America's Pacific Northwest region. Both parents earned their names with their specific, fruity flavors, and gained reputations for their unique highs. Their progeny, Blue Grape #1, appeals to those who select varieties for flavor and prefer an awake, head-focused experience.

Blue Grape #1 combines these connoisseur qualities with easy gardening, thanks to a moderate flowering period of about two months, indoors or out. These plants like to grow large with multiple budding sites. Electric recommends tying larger side branches near the end of flowering to support the buds and keep order in the garden. The leaves are wide and dark with purple-blue coloration on some plants. All plants form glossy resin, which can yield some dense finger hash from rubbing the foliage.

The smooth smoke from Blue Grape #1 has mild lung expansion with a full berry savor and a hint of tangy grapefruit. It is an energizing high good for daytime activities. Medicinally, it offers potential pain reduction without losing mental clarity or motivation.

 70/30

 alert and energizing

 very berry

 58 days indoors
late Sept. outdoors

 ♀ Grapefruit x ♂ Blueberry

 100 g (3 oz.) per large plant indoors
275 g (10 oz.) per plant outdoors

13

Photo: Marco

Blue Pearl

Homegrown Fantaseeds

Homegrown Fantaseed's 2001 Cannabis Cup prizewinner, Blue Haze, is crossed here with a sweetheart female, the Silver Pearl, to produce an enviable plant. Blue Pearl is a tall sativa-like strain with a soft taste and strong high. Indoors, she grows well as a multi-branch plant, but can be tamed with some effort to fit a sea of green growing style.

Blue Pearl forms nice cone-like single colas, compact and picture-perfect rather than the loose clusters sometimes found with sativas or hazes in particular. The minimal foliage is dark green and the leaflets are skinny and finger-like. Blue Pearl's mother, the Silver Pearl, is a fast finishing sativa, balancing out the super long season usually required for a haze. As a result, this plant can be grown outdoors in a wide belt between 45 degrees North and 45 degrees South. Given the grow characteristics of equatorial plants, this variety produces well, with an average 20-25 grams (¾ ounces) from a 70 cm (2-foot) plant.

For those who like an up, nearly psychedelic type of high, Blue Pearl will be a favorite. The flavor is mild with a fresh edge of lemon citrus that cleans the palate. The buzz is a creeper but then the pearly grin kicks in with a trippy tone that provokes new perspectives. Terrific for summertime.

 70/30

 psychedelic

 mild lemon

 60-65 days

 ♀ Silver Pearl x ♂ Blue Haze

 20-25 g (¾ oz.) per plant indoors

 SOG

14

Homegrown Sweet Homegrown

Homegrown Fantaseeds

Homegrown Fantaseeds started in 1997, continuing the genetic lines of one of the first Dutch marijuana seed companies, Positronics. In the 1980s and early '90s, Positronics' mission was to make all the supplies and information needed to grow quality marijuana available in one location. Their intention was to provide a friendly resource and a positive influence on the planet. Homegrown carries the torch, at least when it comes to providing a helpful, approachable staff and quality seeds.

Seeds were originally available at the Homegrown Fantasy coffeeshop, but this was too crowded, so the company owner Jaap opened "Fantaseeds Garden" as a separate seed outlet at Nieuwe Nieuwstraat 25, just around the corner from the coffeeshop. The Homegrown Fantaseeds store is a worthwhile stop on any visit to Amsterdam. In addition to seeds, the shop has a live display garden and carries glassware and bongs, a library of cultivation books and mags, quality items that make unique souvenirs, and of course, seeds—not only Homegrown's own, but those of many other seed companies as well. The employees are happy to discuss seeds, weed, growing and what to do in Amsterdam with anyone who drops by.

Homegrown seeds stand on their own reputation for quality, which spans worldwide and includes prizewinning strains such as Super Crystal, Mango, Caramella and Blue Haze.

A lot has changed in the seed business over the years, but you will still find a "homegrown" attitude when you meet the team that forms Homegrown Fantaseeds. Check out their interactive web site at: www.homegrown-fantaseeds.com. And don't miss their sister coffeeshop, less than a minute's walk around the corner on Nieuwezijds Voorburgwal (87a)—just look for the sign with the mystical eye.

A peek inside the Homegrown Fantaseeds shop.

Brains Choice

KC Brains

 70/30

 intense, stoney

White Widow with Haze floral

56-70 days indoors
63-84 days (end Sept.)
outdoors

♀ Lambsbread Jamaica
(1994) x ♂ White Widow
(1996)

160 g (5¹/₂ oz.) per plant
indoors
up to 900 g (2 lbs.) per plant
outdoors

KC Brains is known for producing some hard-hitting indicas, and this, his Brains Choice, may be the new flagship for the stoney side of his strains. KC grew the mother from seeds given to him by a Jamaican man he met in a coffeshop in Northern Holland. The seeds were Lambsbread, a legendary Jamaican strain, strongly but not purely sativa. KC crossed the Lambsbread with a classic all-indica White Widow from Ingemar, one of the early seed breeders in the Amsterdam scene.

After only one cross, KC spent two years monitoring the new F1 for quality and stability. He was so pleased with the results that he named the hybrid "Brains Choice."

Brains Choice forms a marmalade of white and orange hairs as its flowers mature. The orange comes from the Lambsbread, while the White Widow parentage shows through in the frosty proliferation of trichomes on the bud and nearby leaf. The buds cluster along the branches rather than forming one solid cola at the ends.

KC likes to grow his plants large, and this productive indica-dominant cross is no exception. It's a big plant delivering strong yields with a knockout stone. Growing this strain is not particularly difficult, but does benefit from experience and is less appropriate for a first attempt.

The taste is memorable but difficult to describe—White Widow's airy, sandalwood herbiness accented with a touch of floral haze, mellow and easy on the windpipe. Yet many people will find that one hit is plenty. It may not be the right pot for an after-work "happy hour" toke; it's more suited for sleep or a little mental vacation. Some "blanking out" on the conversation can be expected. While the parent White Widow is considered a creeper, the Lambsbread cross has sped up onset so that the high comes on quick and intense. As KC says, "Open the door, and it's there."

Brains Damage

Even though Brains Damage is a four-way cross, all the parents are indicas, making this strain a very stable, consistent single phenotype plant. The Mexican and Hawaiian strains came from a friend in the North of Holland, while the Mango and KC 636 are part of the strain library Brains has developed over the last decade.

KC selects for strains that grow big to suit outdoor or greenhouse gardens, or indoor gardens when plant count limits may encourage gardeners to grow a few larger plants. KC's big girls deliver a worthwhile yield and remain within the laws in areas where marijuana gardening is restricted but legal.

Brains Damage takes about 2 months to finish outdoors, although KC prefers the stickiness and additional ripeness it gains when allowed to go a full 10 weeks. While this plant forms plenty of bushy foliage, the calyxes develop at a single site, forming tight colas that range from 10 cm (4 inches) to huge meter-long (3 feet) buds in outdoor gardens. This variety does not love the heat and yields more in temperate climates or indoors as long as the temperature stays in pot's comfort zone of 70-80° F. Overall, this variety is a good beginner strain, delivering a rich yield with minimum nutrient supplementation and basic maintenance.

Brain's strains are often knockouts, and the name Brains Damage tells you that this is among KC's heavyweights. The stone kicks in after two or three hits. The mouth dries, the eyelids droop, and knowledgeable onlookers can spot the telltale signs of a powerful indica high. The palate is a little fruity from the Mango and Hawaii parents, with a drier eucalyptus aroma from the Acapulco.

 relaxing, eyedroop

 sage with hint of fruit

 56-70 days indoors
63-84 days (end Sept.) outdoors

 ♀ Acapulco Mexican (1993) x ♂ Hawaiian x ♂ Mango (2001) x ♂ KC 636

 up to 140 g (5 oz.) indoors
up to 800 g (1¾ lbs.) outdoors

 SOG

Brains Escape

KC Brains

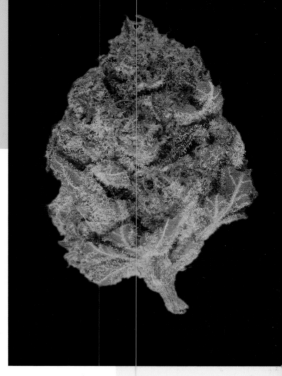

Through the 1990s, Switzerland seemed to be on the verge of a progressive marijuana policy, indeed of becoming the next pot hotspot. KC Brains was among several growers who bred Swiss seeds in anticipation of a more liberal legal climate. Edelweiss is a distinctive Swiss strain that emerged in this period, based on a Swiss indica with a strong local reputation. Unfortunately, the Swiss government retreated from looser cannabis laws and began to crack down on pot culture, especially if it was "imported." Many growers who had tested Switzerland's evolving pot policies were charged as criminals or shown to the border.

KC Brains brought Edelweiss with him back to Holland, where he combined it with KC 606 and a Brazilian strain seasoned with sativa from South Ecuador. The result is a fresh lemon weed whose buzz feels more "high" than "stoned." The Brains Escape pattern of growth is decidedly indica, delivering big plants with incredibly wide, dark, fat leaves. This strain's long growing season rewards outdoor growers who vegetate starter plants indoors or in a greenhouse, and then transplant outside to flower for 9-12 weeks before the frost starts.

This is an enjoyable tasting weed to share with friends. It goes well with playing in the park, going on a hike, or seeing outdoor music shows. A complimentary weed for summer, Brains Escape can also bring back that summer feeling during any season of the year.

I

happy, social

lemon

63-77 days indoors
63-84 days (end Sept.) outdoors

♀ Edelweiss (2000) x
♂ Brazil's Best (2001) x
♂ KC 606 (male)

up to 180 g (6 oz.) per plant indoors
up to 1.2 kilos (2.6 lbs.) per plant outdoors

May Day is Jay Day: The Million Marijuana March
By Ed Rosenthal

Marijuana marches had been going on in New York around May Day for almost thirty years when the Million Marijuana March was conceived. YIPPIE! activist Dana Beal and *High Times* publisher John Holmstrom put their heads together at the Cannabis Cup in Amsterdam—they weren't just sniffing vapors, they were seeking answers like the oracles at Delphi.

The first Million Marijuana March had its headquarters in Dana and John's hometown, New York City, and took place on May 1, 1998. It started at Washington Square Park, snaking down Broadway to Battery Park at the tip of Manhattan. About 25,000 people attended: 18,000 activists and 7,000 police.

As people assembled, it did not look propitious. There were cops in cars and buses, on horseback, in scooters and on foot. It was very intimidating. Would-be supporters were coming down, assessing the situation and leaving. Finally, a half hour late, the march started out of the park, toward Broadway.

Mayor Giuliani's enforcers performed as expected. In one instance they arrested six people in a smoking circle passing a single joint. The police were herding people onto the sidewalk, but our ranks were swelling. As we turned right to follow Broadway's twisted path through lower Manhattan, we kept going past the sidewalk and into the street. At first, law enforcement tried to push us back, but we kept surging, and within a minute or two, the barricades came down and we unfurled our banners.

Thousands of people joined us as we walked down the avenue. One woman told me that she had no idea the event was happening, but once she saw it, she stopped shopping and picked up a sign that read, "I Smoke Pot and I Vote."

"I can shop anytime," she said, "but I've never done anything like this before. I'm glad I'm here."

We crossed into Battery Park and the stage was set up for speakers and music. But

Photo: Ed Rosenthal

Photo: Ed Rosenthal

the words were less significant than the action. In the face of a repressive policy people braved the authorities to start changing the law.

The event has grown from its first year, where a handful of cities participated, to 2004, when there were demonstrations, festivals and rallies in over 300 cities worldwide. In 1999, 40 cities had demonstrations demanding an end to anti-marijuana laws. While the idea originated with international activist and Cures Not Wars founder Dana Beale, events in each city are organized locally and reflect the issues and organizations in each place.

New York's 2004 event had a lower attendance than the average 30,000, but with the new New York mayor, who admitted liking marijuana, there were no arrests.

On the left coast, the 2004 San Francisco rally and celebration was very mellow with virtually no police presence. A new generation of marijuana advocates were joined by several California politicians who spoke in support of removing all penalties for use. In spite of the malign over-presence of the Bush regime, there were victories to report on the battle for California's medical marijuana initiatives and support to make marijuana offenses the lowest priority for law enforcement in many Bay Area cities. The mood was celebratory and there was musical entertainment to keep the good vibe flowing.

The London rally has been produced by Shane Collins of the Green Party since 1999. In 2004, over 100,000 people attended. It has the support of the *London Independent*, a local newspaper. Now it's an incredible event reported on throughout the country.

There is nothing quite like attending the Million Marijuana March wherever you are. Even if there are only a few thousand or even a few hundred people at a local event, the spirit of events happening simultaneously and throughout the day all over the world permeates the air. You can think it, you can feel it, you can breathe in the telltale smell of it and know you are a part of the force for sanity when it comes to cannabis policy.

Find out more: www.millionmarijuanamarch.org

Bronze Whaler

MJOZ

This strain comes from a seed bank formed by three Aussie growers with more than fifty years of cultivation experience between them. All of their strains carry a name with some connection to Australia; Bronze Whaler is named for a tropical whaler shark found off the southern coast. Often shortened to "Bronzie," the shark's name comes from its recognizable bronze sheen. Bronze Whalers grow about 6-8 feet in length and often feed close to shore where they sometimes mistakenly attack swimmers.

This indica-based namesake plant produces dense compact buds with an abundance of fine white pistils that change to a bronze hue on maturity. The leaves are serrated with a tapered angular shape not unlike a shark fin. When the buds ripen, the leaves lose vitality and change to a yellow-brown.

This F3 strain is a solid producer that reaches around 4 feet in height when flowered at 12 inches. It does well in a sea of green due to its columnar shape that allows for a good yield when the plant is pruned to one main stem. MJOZ like to use a coco/perlite mix as medium.

Bronze Whaler is an evening smoke, not well suited for daytime or work-time activities. The length of the high averages 3-4 hours with smokers often glued to the sofa for the duration. Bronze Whaler has medicinal potential for relieving pain and stress. The aroma and taste of this strain are strongly fruity with a distinct tropical overtone, a hint of its South Pacific origins. Bronze Whaler was awarded 2nd Place at the Sydney Cannabis Cup in 2002.

 80/20

 couch lock

 fruity/tropical

 42 days

 ♀ Bronze Whaler x ♂ Skunk #1

 30-40 g (1-1½ oz.) dry cured buds per plant

 SOG

MJOZ on the Bronze Whaler

Until recent times, Australia has been isolated from the cannabis genetics that have been readily available in Europe and North America. During the 1970s, we relied on traveling hippies and surfers to bring the odd seed back home, but there was never enough to filter down to all, so their influence remained limited to single growers and breeders here and there. The importation from Asia and Africa of those now-rare landrace genes, like Thai Buddha and Durban Poison, also failed to generate any stock of seeds in the Australian scene.

From the late 1980s on, growers began little by little to import seed stock from overseas seedbanks. Now, since the Internet has brought instant access, all and sundry have enthusiastically jumped on the bandwagon.

It was in this context that the Bronze Whaler emerged. Some eager growers planted a mix of Afghani, White Widow and Cali O that they imported. A male Cali O went unnoticed, and created some seeds that were collected. From the subsequent seed-grow, a plant we called "Bronze" was isolated and clones were kept.

The Bronze Whaler is an F3 hybrid of this Bronze female, which was crossed with a Super Skunk male. Four years of selective backcrossing allowed us to isolate traits we liked from the Bronze female. Bronze Whaler retains its mother's exceptional aroma and taste, but has a higher overall yield. So far, the Bronze Whaler has only been grown indoors, but has proven adaptable to all media. It is an easy plant to grow, and thrives in hydro setups. Bronze Whaler is a terrific example of what can happen when we mix global with local—we've expanded the gene pool in one of the world's primo cannabis gardening spots without losing track of what makes Aussie weed a specialty worth experiencing.

Photo: Donja

California Grapefruit

DNA Genetics

You can take the genetics out of California but you can't take the California out of the genetics. The guys from DNA are Southern California natives who migrated to realize their calling as breeders in the relative weed freedom of Amsterdam. But they didn't leave all the great Cali genetics behind. California Grapefruit combines three of the Golden State's favorite indicas: Northern Lights, Skunk #1 and Afghani.

This plant autoflowers, with a short growing season of 7½ to 9 weeks. A heavy yielder, she is a perfect choice for gardeners with space issues. Since she naturally forms one mega-cola and few side branches, California Grapefruit almost volunteers for sea of green planting. Manicuring California Grapefruit is a breeze. She tends to stay small, averaging 2½ feet at maturity if vegetated for 2 weeks prior to flowering, but her big colas amount to at least one ounce of dried bud per plant, on average.

California Grapefruit's high creeps up, then settles in for hours. Her heritage of world-class indicas offers a classic "body high" that eases the mind and muscles like a long day lounging by the pool. Sleep often follows. This might be a good weed to relieve insomnia and tension. The smoke both smells and tastes a bit like a grapefruit plucked from a California orchard, a mixture of tart citrus, dirt and sun.

 relaxing

 grapefruit

 52-63 days

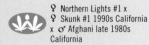 ♀ Northern Lights #1 x ♀ Skunk #1 1990s California x ♂ Afghani late 1980s California

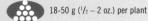 18-50 g (½ – 2 oz.) per plant

 SOG

24

Candy Cane Brain

Shadow Seed Co.

Candy Cane Brain descends from a series of crossings starting from Brain Strain, the anchor of Shadow Seeds' breeding program. Shadow first crossed Brain Strain with a bud-heavy Blueberry-Northern Lights hybrid and then backcrossed the offspring with Brain Strain. The resulting strain, called Silver Shadow, raises the hybrid line's indica quotient and its bud-to-leaf ratio. The final step in Candy Cane Brain's fruit juicy pedigree is a cross between a Silver Shadow mother and the well known British Columbian strain, Grapefruit.

Candy Cane Brain can be cultivated compactly as a single branch sea of green or will also lend itself to multi-branching, where each branch becomes a site for nice tight buds with minimal foliage. A few weeks into budding, Candy Cane Brain often elongates and will need to be staked by week 3 or 4. At maturity, crystals coat even the large fan leaves of Candy Cane Brain, giving off an aroma so sweet that it can tempt the lightweight or occasional toker.

Some flavor-bred pot tastes as if wine or fruit juice had splashed its foliage and then dried, bringing forward the fruit sugars. For Candy Cane Brain, it's a splash of berry and citrus over savory skunk. The breeders say that first-time smokers of Candy Cane Brain may find themselves rolling an extra joint simply for the taste. The high is giddy and disorienting, with a certain degree of brain freeze at onset. However, once you get back into the pace of the conversation, Candy Cane Brain is a good social catalyst for parties and other fun situations.

 80/20

 social, mind numbing at first

 fruity, hint of skunk

 56 days

 Silver Shadow x Grapefruit

 100 g (3 oz.) per large plant indoors
275 g (10 oz.) per plant outdoors

 SOG

Photo: Donja

Cannalope Haze

DNA Genetics

"cut-through," heady

melon with hint of haze

58-65 days indoors
end Oct. outdoor in California

Haze brothers backcrossed
into Michoacan sativa

20-40 g (³/₄-1¹/₂ oz.)
per plant

Cannalope Haze is the sativa gardener's ideal synthesis. DNA began with a quality sativa, then backcrossed and selected to achieve a shorter season and higher yield than is typical of these equatorial natives. This plant has pure sativa roots with a hint of haze mixed in, and finishes in a speedy 8-9 weeks. Outdoors, she finishes at the end of October when grown in California, or other Mediterranean, wine-growing type of climates. Colder and darker climates may mean a later finish.

The physiognomy of this plant is typically one main cola with small side branches, so unlike many sativas, Cannalope Haze can be cultivated in a sea of green style. The average height is 1 to 1.5 meters (3-5 feet). DNA prefers soil over hydroponic methods for Cannalope.

The average plant will deliver about ³/₄ ounces when flowered after a two-week vegetative period. The buds are tight and compact with very thin leaves. She stays light green throughout her cycle. Trichome frost appears early in flowering, but patient growers will be rewarded if they allow Cannalope to reach a full meter of height before they start harvesting.

The smell of this variety when properly cured is reminiscent of fresh-cut cantaloupe with a hint of haze aftertaste. Cannalope Haze also has a suprising intensity for a sativa. DNA calls it a "cut-through" high, meaning that smoking the Cannalope Haze usually makes its unique qualities felt, even cutting through a pre-existing buzz. Indeed, the potency may "floor" some smokers, and for most it is probably best to save this pot for an afternoon 4:20 smoke or for later in the evening unless it is a special wake-and-bake occasion.

DNA Genetics: from Lala-land to the Netherlands

The DNA boys started growing marijuana in the late 1980s in a small city in the greater Los Angeles region: Hollyweed! Over the next ten years they experimented with seeds from all over the world, fascinated with the diversity in this one special plant. When friends would go on travels, the only souvenir these boys wanted were seeds. They grew short and long season varieties: from a 21-week haze pure sativa to a Himalayan strain that autoflowered, finishing in only 6½ weeks.

By the mid-1990s, California was getting hot. Even with Proposition 215, California's medical marijuana initiative, in full effect, there were no guarantees. The battle between state and the federal government moved the front line of the drug war to California, and put patients and growers directly in the line of fire.

These boys had collected, catalogued and cultivated some incredible strains. They knew their love of cultivation and breeding contributed to cannabis culture, but at home these skills were being rewarded with arrest, trials and jail time. It was time to lay low or change venues. They decided to go for it, and made the leap across the pond, settling in Holland by early 2002.

In this little big city of relative marijuana freedom, it was tough to be the new expats on the block. They struggled through, and with help from a few brotherly breeders, they got on their feet. Now all their seed company needed was a name. A friend had taken to calling this growing duo "D and A," after the initials of their first names. While searching their brains for a good name, this friend jokingly called them by this nickname and a light bulb went off: DNA—how simple! Plants come down to DNA, their special genetics!

After 15 years of breeding and collecting strains, the DNA breeders now are just beginning to come into their own. In 2004, DNA placed 3rd in the IC 420 Cup (sativa category) with Cannalope Haze, and hash made from another DNA strain, the California Grapefruit, took 1st place at the same event.

DNA is grateful to Soma, Bonguru and Big A , as well as all the residents of Amsterdam who helped them get their footing. And last but not least, they thank all of their silent partners out there all over the world, keeping the culture alive and growing.

CannaSutra

Delta-9 Labs

CannaSutra is the flagship strain of Delta-9 Labs. This F1 hybrid has a good yield, a sweet aroma and a stimulating sativa high that retains the lucidity of its Reclining Buddha parent.

While a stronger indoor performer, this strain can also be grown outdoors in moderate to hot climates. She likes lots of food, but is sensitive to overwatering. CannaSutra can be super cropped with ease, and flowers in just under 10 weeks, putting on tremendous girth in the final two weeks. Its lime-green buds are loose and airy until the last week, when they harden and the calyxes swell with resin. The typical yield, about an ounce per square foot, seems to be consistent across growing methods, but this plant performs best when given root space and room space to develop multiple branches.

CannaSutra's mild yet mood elevating high tends to boost mental focus rather than derailing it, making this a good all-day smoke. It is particularly appropriate for those who like to toke when they sit down for a session of computer or graphic work, or for getting philosophical with friends. The strain's name – from the Sanskrit love manual *Kama Sutra* – also suggests profound explorations between lovers. The smoke is incense-like—sweet, aromatic, and soft. Some users report strong bronchial dilation, which may alleviate asthma and related conditions.

 I S 70/30

 clear-headed, uplifting

 distinctly sweet

 58-65 days indoors end Oct. outdoors in California

 ♀ Reclining Buddha x ♂ Sensi Star

 300-500 g/m² (1 - 1½ oz./ft.²) indoors

Photos: Bobby B.

Cherry Pez Livity (CPL) ▬

Apothecary

Cherry Pez Livity (CPL) was bred to incorporate Livity's outstanding yield and extreme branching patterns with the indica father's mold resistance and general hardiness in cold climates. A relatively short plant, CPL finishes in 8–9 weeks when grown indoors.

CPL does well in both soil and hydro conditions. The typical indoor yield is between 1½–2½ ounces per multi-branch plant. When grown with a large pot and longer vegetation period, individual indoor plants can yield up to 7 ounces. Sea of green cultivation is feasible, but given CPL's predilection for branching, the garden must be monitored for overcrowding and pruned fastidiously.

Outdoors, she has been successfully grown at latitudes of 48–50 degrees. (This is the latitude of Vancouver, in southern Canada, or Geneva, in Switzerland.) At these lattitudes, CPL plants finish at the end of September or beginning of October and yield around 2 pounds per plant. At lower latitudes, or when vegged indoors prior to outdoor exposure, CPL has reached 10 feet in height and delivered over 5 pounds from a single plant.

Apothecary strives to keep a natural environment, and enjoys the smooth freshness that results when organic methods are used. The Cherry Pez Livity has a fruity bouquet that is just spicy enough to make your mouth water. The taste is spicier than the smell and delivers a mind wandering high with a soothing, body-unlocking feel, great to put the work week behind or to enhance the enjoyment of being out in nature.

 60/40

 wandering mind, relaxing

 fruity/hint of spice

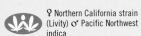 58-65 days

 ♀ Northern California strain (Livity) ♂ Pacific Northwest indica

 1000 g (2 lb.) outdoors

SOG

30

Cinderella 99

Gypsy Nirvana

 SI

 uplifting, giggly

 pineapple

 50-60 days

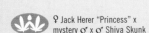 ♀ Jack Herer "Princess" x mystery ♂ x ♂ Shiva Skunk

 50 g (2 oz.) per plant in 11 liter (3 gal.) pot

Cinderella 99 received her name because, like the well-known fairly tale heroine, she is a high-class girl with humble origins. Originally, the Brothers Grimm developed the F1 generation of Cinderella 99, but they discontinued their business, making the strain unavailable. Gypsy Nirvana commissioned the breeders at Nirvana to produce the F2 generation. They selected two top parents and concentrated on reviving a version of Cinderella that retained the "traits package" of delicious flavor, sativa high, and a quick finish.

The F2 Cindy was selected and stabilized. When planted in an 11-liter (3-gallon) soil bucket, Cinderella 99 yields 50 grams (almost 2 ounces) of dried bud on average—not a huge cornucopia of pot yield, but a respectable-sized harvest of premium slow-smoking buds. Cinderella's bud construction is very dense for a sativa-dominant plant, with a fruity aroma and a nice sugary resin coating. Gypsy Nirvana's stabilized F2 Cindys finished flowering between 57 and 61 days under a 12/12 indoor light cycle. Although developed for indoor growing, Cinderella has fared very well outdoors too, yielding of up to one kilo of bud per plant.

The abundance of fine leaves typical of sativas can make Cinderella 99 difficult to manicure, but she is easy to clone. Abundant trichome development can be seen two thirds of the way down her first leaves, closest to the buds.

Cinderella 99 gives a silly, bubbly, yet lucid head high with a few inhalations of her pineapple-like smoke or vapor. Sweet taste and giggle fits make Cindy 99 fun for occasional smokers while her classic sativa mind stimulation – and her good growing traits – will please the old school congregation of devoted tokers.

A Cinderella Story

As told by Mr. Soul of the now defunct Brothers Grimm

Cinderella's Story begins in 1997, when I discovered a few surprising seeds in a bud of Jack Herer (a Sensi strain named after the famous hemp activist) that I bought from the Sensi Smile coffeeshop. I wasn't really expecting much when I grew them, but one of those seeds produced an undeniably special female. I called her "Princess."

I'd also bought some seeds on purpose during the same trip to Sensi Smile, and from these I got a few more promising females and several males. I used pollen from one of these males on a heavy-yielding, dense, resinous Shiva Skunk female (from Sensi Seedbank), then used the resulting seeds to grow a crew of males worthy of crossing with Princess.

At this point, I began the cubing process. I crossed one of the males with Princess, making seeds that were 50% Princess, or P50. I then used males that grew from this batch of P50 seeds to backcross with the original Princess, creating a P75 (75% Princess) batch of seeds. I again backcrossed the original Princess with pollen from a P75 male to get a P88, then once more to get a P94, which is "Cinderella," a cubed version of Princess.

C99 is the F2 generation of this Cinderella plant that Brothers Grimm developed. True-breeding reliability is something that takes a while to prove itself, but the F2 generation of C99 is very much the same as the original F1 C99 in my experience. I feel, but can't say for certain, that subsequent generations will continue to produce plants with the essential traits of the original C99. That's the theory of cubing.

Aside from her stability, Cindy 99 stands out because she finishes flowering in under 60 days, like an indica, but delivers a delicious and pleasurable sativa high. This makes her attractive to both the commercial grower and the cannabis connoisseur.

Cinderella 99 F2s are available in the Gypsy Nirvana Collection at www.seedsdirect.to.

Danky Doodle

KC Brains

 90/10

 stoney

 fruity/ sweet

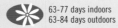 63-77 days indoors
63-84 days outdoors

 ♂ Viking (1990) x ♀ Big Buds
(1993) x ♂ KC 636

 up to 300 g/m² (1 oz/ft.²)
indoors
1.5 kilos (3 lbs.) outdoors

Originally, this indica-ruled variety was referred to as "Double D"—because these ladies very simply had gigantic Dolly Parton-sized buds. KC decided the name needed to be more distinct from Double Dutch, another popular variety that Double D could easily be confused for, but he wanted to stay with the double D theme. He renamed the variety "Danky Doodle" when some visiting American friends suggested it. They said that's what they called really good weed when they were in school in California.

Few people can say the name with a straight face (especially after they've smoked some). Besides sounding goofy, Danky "grows like an imbecile" (as KC says) into the classic Christmas-tree shape with one big cola lump crowning the central branch. Danky's leaves get super dark and the smell gets deep and pungent as the plant matures. Outdoor plants will grow to impressive heights, flowering in mid-July and ready for harvest in the first few weeks of September—a short 7-8 week growing cycle. Indoors, KC recommends 9 plants per square meter (1 plant per square foot). Homegrowers may find that as few as 4-5 plants deliver enough of a yield to keep them in supply.

Danky Doodle's Viking father was given to KC by a Ukrainian friend who came bearing seeds to Holland by way of Zaire. KC crossed the strong Viking indica with Big Buds, a variety from the tasty and productive Mango gene-line. Then he crossed the Viking/Big Buds hybrid with his library strain KC 636 to maintain the genetics of the aging 636 seeds in a live lineage. In short, Danky Doodle turns out to be a "melting pot" of global indica genes for a classic sigh-of-relief body stone. The Mango and KC 636 crossings add increased yield, a nice growth of frost, and a sweet fruit-butter palate.

Diamond Head

Sagarmatha

Diamond Head is the name of the large volcano that glimmers like a jewel on Oahu's emerald skyline. Held in "High Esteem" by the locals, honored by the chiefs, and enjoyed by anyone with an appreciation for Mother Nature's beauty, Diamond Head evokes the vision of what Sagarmatha believes to be her version of primo pakalolo.

To make Diamond Head, a mother Flow plant was crossed with an atypical Flow male that exhibited a Hawaiian phenotype. Diamond Head displays a mostly sativa growth pattern—slender serrated purple leaves and elongated purple buds plump with sticky crystalline trichomes. Everything about this plant is sativa except for the large, dense flower tops and spongy buds, which have a slight indica profile.

Diamond Head would love to grow on the tropical mountainsides of Hawaii, but any garden where plants can continue to ripen into mid or late October will suffice. For indoor growing, Sagarmatha prefers soil. Sea of green or clipping and branching are both viable approaches. Many of her big, lovely buds can be picked early. The buds are usually the diameter of a large broom handle and about 8-20 cm (3-8 inches) in length with a heavy, bread-like density. The plants reach 6-8 feet outdoors, 3-5 feet indoors, and can be harvested twice in regions with long growing seasons.

Hawaii's mountain forests smell of clean wet greenery with a hint of hibiscus and pineapple. This is also a good description of Diamond Head's palate. The high comes on smooth and easy, with a feeling of mental peacefulness but not physical lethargy. Diamond Head suits tokers who wish to remain active and creative; programmers, musicians and especially romantics are among those who benefit from Diamond Head's pleasures.

 S I

 cerebral, calm

 sweet/fruity

 55 - 60 days

 ♀ Flow x ♂ atypical Flow

 300 - 350 g/m² (1-1¼ oz./ft.²) dried, indoors

 SOG

Double Dutch

Magus Genetics

Photos: Green Born Identity

Double Dutch mixes the genetics of the Warlock male with a pre-2000 Chronic female, two popular native Dutch varieties. The Warlock—Magus Genetics' foundation strain—is a branchy plant with a pleasurable scent. Chronic, a strain developed by Serious Seeds in the 1990s, forms massive colas. Their offspring, Double Dutch, shows its indica pedigree by developing fat leaves, thick stems, and a bushy growth pattern during its seedling and vegetative stages. In the flowering stage, this variety produces giant sativa-like buds similar to elongated popcorn balls.

Bred for indoor gardens, Double Dutch performs well in bio, coco and hydro growth mediums, but hydro is recommended if yield is the main objective. Large gardens allow multi-branching, but staking is necessary due to Double Dutch's willowy branches and weighty flowers. However, when a relatively small number of plants are grown, the growth pattern tends to be shorter and much less lateral. Therefore, sea of green is possible with a smaller garden, but is still not the most productive setup.

Most taste buds will appreciate the pleasant fruity wildflower flavor that is also apparent in the scent. The buzz is complex and strong with both cerebral and bodily components. It starts in the mind and slowly flows down the torso into a more body-centered buzz that is lazy, but not sleepy. This buzz allows one to drift in its sensation for 2-4 hours depending on tolerance level.

 60/40

 mentally relaxing first, then lazy body feeling

 wildflower/fruit

 55-65 days

 ♀ Chronic (pre-2000) x ♂ Warlock

 350-600 g/m² (1-2 oz./ft.²)

U.S. Festivals & Fairs

By Ed Rosenthal

Seattle Hempfest
Usually the 3rd weekend in August

The Seattle Hempfest is the marijuana movement in evolution. It started as a handful of volunteers producing a small hemp exposition, inspired by Jack Herer's book, *The Emperor Wears No Clothes*. This seminal book on hemp explores its history and many uses, and links the criminalization of sister plants marijuana and hemp to collusion between various industries and the criminal justice system.

In 1992, Hempfest's second year, 2,000 people celebrated in Volunteer Park. The political nature of the event was clearly denoted by the placement of two large sinsemilla plants on the stage.

By 1995, over 50,000 attendees celebrated at Myrtle Edwards Park, located on the waterfront. They were greeted by an incredible line-up of speakers, including Jack Herer, activist Chris Conrad and U.S. federal marijuana patient Elvy Musikka. The police also attended for the first time, both making arrests and handing out numerous citations for marijuana "offenses."

Photo: Ed Rosenthal

In 2001 the event expanded from a single day to the entire weekend. Attendance was estimated at over 150,000. Police relented in their efforts to arrest or cite for marijuana offenses and instead adopted a cooperative stance, helping organizers with the large crowds and vendor support. Fittingly, the theme that year was "No Prison For Pot."

In 2003, with over 200,000 in attendance, Hempfest drew celebrities such as Woody Harrelson, NFL star Mark Stepnoski, and TV host Rick Steves in addition to the top brass of the activist organizations.

The Seattle Hempfest is a spectacular event. It is truly a celebration of the culture, a space where marijuana is embraced in sharp contrast to society's rules. The festival celebrates the culture with great music and entertainment, excellent healthy food, vendors galore, passionate speakers and a virtual mushroom cloud of smoke at 4:20.

Seattle Hempfest proves that culture and politics do mix. The great peace leader, Abbie Hoffman defined his politics as "Revolution for the Fun of It." The Hempfest is an actualization of that statement.

Find out more: www.hempfest.org

Boston Freedom Rally
Usually third Saturday in September—Boston, Massachusetts

Boston Commons is an historical center of American politics. So it's altogether fitting that cannabis aficionados should rally here to protest and petition the government for a redress of grievances. The Commons is a large park in the middle of Boston and it has many entrances so it can easily hold a very large group of people. This gives people the space to listen to speeches and music from the stage, picnic in the park or walk along the walkways lined with vendors selling hemp and marijuana-related products, including hemp foods and hemp seed oils products, clothing, books and more.

The festival was started in 1989 by the Massachusetts NORML chapter, known as Mass CANN, with only 250 people attending. Over the past 15 years total attendance has grown to an estimate of over 50,000 people. At its peak there are probably 20,000 people in the park.

The festival speakers list is a veritable Who's Who of marijuana activism. In 2003 Keith Stroup, Ethan Nadelman and Ed Rosenthal were speakers. In other years Jack Herer, Kevin Zeese, John Sinclair, Dennis Peron, Don Wirtshafter have all spoken at the cradle of U.S. independence.

Before the eighth rally, police searched people coming into the park only for weapons and alcohol. They tolerated marijuana smoking. In 1996 police policy changed and they started to make arrests. Since that time the police presence has increased incrementally. I was surprised to see a police arrest tent perhaps 100 feet stage left. More than 75 people were arrested in 2003 at the rally simply for lighting up.

Jim Scales, attending the rally from Asheville North Carolina, and composer of the song "Overgrow the Government", wrote, "Most of those arrested would fit this basic profile: 18-24 years old, male, white, no prior criminal record. The circumstances of their arrests were identical: each was observed in possession of marijuana by undercover police. Each arrestee's only threat to the public safety was having plant matter in their pocket. The devil's weed.

"The papers tomorrow will say that 55 people were arrested for marijuana possession and/or distribution. No one was arrested for anything else. There were no fights, thefts, or cries for help. No blood was shed, no paramedic services needed. No overdoses. No weapons of mass destruction."

One protester, John Holmes, snapped photos of undercover narcs with his picture camera and sent the photo with a voice message to others at the rally. Soon the undercover agents photos were published all over the phone system.

Even with the police presence the rally is still a great event and well worth attending. Just don't bring smokeables. Eat a brownie or use some tincture sublingually. Then you can turn on right in front of Boston's police and they won't even know. Yes it's a great day for them too. Overtime, a day in the sun, and a body count with little chance of violence.

Find more info on this event: www.masscann.org/rally.htm

Photo: Bill Downing

The Great Midwest Harvest Festival
Usually in October—Madison, Wisconsin

The Great Midwest Harvest Festival follows the traditional fall harvest-time celebration of abundance. Started in 1971, this event was first billed as The Madison Smoke-In. Its name change took place in 1985, when it became more of a regional event. At its peak in the late 1980s, it drew up to 25,000. As more events like it sprang up in the Midwest, it has become more state-focused.

At the library mall on the campus of the University of Wisconsin, where the rally first starts, there seem to be so few people. Wisconsin's October weather has already picked up a chill. But after a musical prologue, the first speakers of the day address a crowd, which has grown to several thousand people by late morning.

This healthy mix of students and townies proceeds in a peaceful, parade-like march up State Street to the State Capitol, perhaps a mile away. This march and rally is the main event, a show

Photo: Ed Rosenthal

of numbers who agree that a saner cannabis policy is needed. It is at the capitol steps and the wide streets that surround it where the political turns to celebratory. After about an hour, the rally part of the event ends, but the day is far from over. Most of the crowd moves on to other events, which vary from year to year. There have been parties at clubs, private parties, picnics and even a concert.

The Harvest Festival is a mellow event and there is usually no friction with the authorities, including the police, who are often totally absent. This is not a smoke-free event.

Ben Masel, former YIPPIE! and founder of the festival, said, " Its purpose is to restrain local enforcement and to attract candidates for office, which is part of why it's held in October –with a view toward influencing the election; also because it coincides with the harvest."

Wisconsin is one of the most lenient states and Madison one of the most progressive towns for marijuana in the country. The festival has played a role in electing several cannabis-friendly politicians including Tammy Baldwin, who is now in the House of Representatives. It has also spurred events in other states including neighboring Illinois and Minnesota.

For more info: www.weedstock.com

Ann Arbor Hash Bash
Usually first Saturday in April—Ann Arbor, Michigan

The Ann Arbor Hash Bash has always been a very intense and political event. The very first Hash Bash was in 1972. Early on, the University of Michigan tried to end the rallies but was rebuffed by the courts. The consequent publicity gave it notoriety, and in the years that followed, it drew crowds from all over the Midwest.

The university and the city of Ann Arbor has continued to oppose the festival over the years. Rick Burkett, the founder and long-time organizer of the event, fought for his right to assemble on the campus, and the event has always featured high-powered

Keith Stroup addresses the Hash Bash crowd. Photo: Chad Man

speakers. Adam Brook, the current organizer, carries on the tradition.

The Hash Bash is billed as a Smoke-In—that is, as a rally that condones civil disobedience, considering it a patriotic act taken against despotic laws. It has a police presence and participants who inhale risk arrest. In 2003, six people were cuffed and carried off for asserting their rights in opposition to the laws.

Cops and other official types may even try to tread on unquestioned liberties to intimidate the naive. One year when I was helping set up at the University of Michigan Commons a college cop came up to me and said, "You can't display literature like that here." I said, "I have permission." The cop said, "Who gave it to you?" I replied, "The First Amendment of the Constitution." He walked on.

The Bash, typically held on the first Saturday of April, draws a mixed age crowd of 3,000–4,000 people.

Find out more: www.hashbash.com

Dreadlock

Joint Doctor's High-Bred Seeds

Dreadlock is an even combination of the sativa and indica spectrum that can be recommended for beginning growers. This strain exhibits two phenotypes. One is a slightly fluffy plant with popcorn buds while the other exhibits less branching, denser buds, and fewer small nodules that protrude from the buds. Both types are not as bushy as most sativa-influenced hybrids, and each sprouts a large main cola that looks like a giant nappy dread.

This variety does not need high levels of fertilizer to produce large, heavy buds. It is very hardy and resistant to molds and pests. Joint Doctor prefers to grow this primarily indoor plant in organic soil, but Dreadlock will do well in hydro too. Yields will be slightly better if each plant is given at least one square foot of space, but the formation of one large main cola makes it suitable for sea of green. The best method for this variety is "screen of green."

Dreadlock's dark nine-pronged fan leaves are accessorized with small, distinctively horn-shaped leaflets tucked in at their bases. Her hairs don't really go red when mature but just shrivel up and disappear. The fan leaves turn yellow and drop before harvest, which means little manicuring is required. Dreadlock clones sprout roots and bushy foliage very quickly, making it a great strain for breeding mothers.

Smart growers give Dreadlock a full 9 weeks before harvest, since her buds gain a lot of weight and THC in the final weeks. Once harvested, these super sticky buds produce a very energetic high that creeps up, strengthening over the first half-hour to a psychedelic, slightly speedy feeling. This mildly musky variety is great for socializing and known for its "giggle stick" qualities. Dreadlock is also a good variety for the hash lover.

 50/50

 creeper, social, energetic

 sweet & musky

 60-65 days indoors
mid-Oct. outdoors at 46 N

 ♀ equatorial sativa x
♂ Middle Eastern indica

 400-500 g/m² (1⅓-1⅔
oz./ft.²) with 1 plant per ft.²

 SOG

45

Ducksfoot

Wally Duck

I S

smiley, functional

spicy coffee cinnamon

60-72 days

♀ Ducksfoot x ♂ sativa
backcrossed to 97%
Ducksfoot

200 g - 1 kilo (7 oz.-2 lbs.)
per plants

Ducksfoot is named for its unique leaves, which have webbing between the leaflets, evoking the feet of waterfowl, rather than the fingerlike morphology of the leaves that has become one of the most recognizable icons to identify pot.

In Australia, Ducksfoot is an outdoor variety only. This strain seems more at home in warmer climates that don't suffer frosts too early. Several outdoor grows in temperate regions of the Northern hemisphere showed good growth but the quantity and quality of the buds were poor when compared with its native climate of Australia.

Ducksfoot is a large growing plant that likes to get its feet in the soil and spread its roots to support branching. Wally Duck grows this strain in a natural sea of green, for both stealth purposes and increased yield. It is a very heavy feeder and will take all the fertilizer you care to give it—nearly double the amount most plants prefer.

As the plants mature, the odd leaves spread out, some reaching the size of dinner plates. Wally prunes to 4-6 main branches, bending them to create a predominantly horizontal profile, with as little vertical growth as possible. Without pruning, Ducksfoot shows extensive branching patterns. Many plants display attractive pink pistils as they ripen. In favorable climates, outdoor yields are rich —200 grams and up per plant.

Ducksfoot's odor is noticeable at several meters' distance from the plant. Although it is a complex smell not immediately identifiable as "pot," it can still sabotage attempts at stealth. The extreme aroma carries over into the taste: a strong spicy coffee taste that lingers pleasantly on the tongue after exhaling, sometimes with a cinnamon aftertaste. The buzz is a smile-inducing euphoria that doesn't sacrifice coherency, making it a great daytime toke for socializing or working in the garden.

Ducksfoot & Camouflage

The unique webbing found between the leaflets on the Ducksfoot variety is a boon for camouflage gardening. The trait originated with this variety's mostly-indica mother. She was crossed with a male sativa, and then inbred, selecting for the webbing trait in each generation. Now all seeds grown from this stabilized indica/sativa mix will deliver the same surprising leaf structure.

All cannabis forms fingered leaflets before flowering. Ducksfoot's first leaves appear large and wedge-shaped, then they spread into a three-fingered pattern connected by webs – picture a duck's foot and you have it. When this strain flowers, the leaves thin out somewhat and the webbing seems less pronounced in the last stages of growth.

Ducksfoot is a rangy, vigorous plant. It buds in impressive columns that can reach several feet in length. Once the monster colas appear with their powerful smell, Ducksfoot's identity may be obvious, but the atypical leaves can make amateur visitors to the garden ask themselves whether this plant is indeed pot. Especially when trained toward horizontal growth, the non-spiky, non-serrated foliage can hinder identification from a distance.

Other strains with good stealth traits include Joint Doctor's Lowryder (p. 80), which grows so short that it's easy to hide, and Biddy Early (p. 6), which can be trained to grow like a vine. Strains like these have a potential advantage in outdoor gardens since they don't quite match the profile that alerts cops and robbers, the most serious pests for any grow.

Dutch Treat x Northern Lights

East Island Seed Co.

Dutch Treat, the mother side of this cross, is an 80% indica—a strong, dark pot with sticky solid tops, a sweetly orange bite and a stimulant stone. The father, Northern Lights, is a potent, relaxing indica, prized by hybrid breeders for its stability and fast cycle. Thus the DT/NL cross appeals to indica fans and pragmatic gardeners. Even in its home region, the rainy coasts of British Columbia, DT x NL is productive, hardy, and finishes flowering in only 7 weeks.

Once established, this plant's rapid growth can be easily seen from one day to the next. DT x NL leaves are thin and may turn purplish at ripening. Branches are bendy and may need to be tied up as the heavy buds can pull them down. Still, multi-branch plants are good yielders in this strain, producing many large, resinous tops.

In the great outdoors, this plant typically reaches a height of 4-6 feet. A 5-foot tall outdoor plant produces up to 8 ounces, with individual buds weighing as much as a half-ounce each. When grown small in the "sea of green" method, yields of at least 2 ounces per plant can be expected.

Dutch Treat x Northern Lights equals a potent and fairly alert indica high. The stone comes on quite slowly but strengthens to a full-on buzz that most people find functional when there is no heavy thinking required. However, this variety may also creep up to a couch-lock level, requiring a little time-out to recover a more social and functional state of mind. It can be a great aid to getting some restful time. DT x NL retains the fruity savor of its mother, with a distinct lean toward the citrus.

70/30

creeper/awake

fruity/possibly citrus

50 days indoors
mid-Sept. outdoors

♀ Dutch Treat x
♂ Northern Lights

2 oz. per plant (SOG) indoors
5 oz. per plant outdoors

SOG

Early Sativa

Great White North

Great White North is a small company whose specialty is outdoor varieties for Canadian seasons. They describe themselves as "a commercial grower that got carried away" into seed science. Their straightforwardly named Early Sativa is exactly that: a short-season equatorial acclimated to summers in Canada's great outdoors.

Early Sativa performs well in nearly all outdoor settings, finishing on the Canadian prairies at the end of August. Early Sativa grows into the traditional Christmas-tree shape with a large central cola. This plant's physiognomy is strongly sativa, with light green tones and long thin leaves, but Early Sativa stays fairly diminutive, with an average height between 2 and 4 feet. Despite the manageable size and central bud formation, this plant is best suited as a multi-branch. She would yield less if crowded into a sea of green. The buds are unexpectedly compact given this plant's pure sativa lineage. Gardeners can expect an average yield of 150 grams (5 ounces) per plant, and a possible 300 grams with good fertilization and an early start.

Early Sativa brings an enjoyable fresh sunkissed fruitiness to the palate. Occasional or light smokers will appreciate this strain's easy ride into an enjoyably lucid high, mild and easy to regulate. Early Sativa enhances work or play, especially hikes, picnics, gardening or with a glass of wine and the company of friends.

mellow, functional

fruity

end Aug. in Canada

sativa

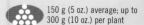
150 g (5 oz.) average; up to 300 g (10 oz.) per plant

Early Swazi Skunk

Greenthumb Seeds

S

mellow/euphoric

floral

mid-late Sept. in SE Ontario when planted in mid-May

♀ Swazi Skunk x
♂ Swazi Skunk

200-400 g (7-14 oz.) per plant

Early Swazi Skunk is eastern Canada's answer to a short-season pure sativa for outdoor growers. This variety was originally brought from South Africa, where Dr. Greenthumb first experienced its well-rounded "smooth" psychoactivity. It has not been crossed with any other varieties, but kept pure and inbred, merely selecting over many generations for the characteristics of improved yield and early finishing.

Originally, sativas are equatorial plants. Conventional wisdom would limit outdoor growing in Canada to indicas, but Early Swazi Skunk has been acclimated to the north over many generations, so that now she offers outstanding outdoor growth and yield as far north as Ontario (50-52 degrees North latitude). This is true even when the seeds are started outdoors. The breeder adds that Early Swazi Skunk is "no dog indoors" either, producing decent sativa yields with multi-branch gardening. Early Swazi Skunk may be a good candidate for screen of green.

This sativa's branches are frond-like, reaching lengths between 3 and 6 feet. Early Swazi Skunk's few leaves are delicate and narrow and the flower-to-leaf ratio is very high. More flowers means more light nectar in the dried bud's palate, a sweet aroma, and a great yield (up to 400 grams per plant outdoors).

Early Swazi Skunk kisses the mind with a smooth, peaceful buzz, euphoric but not overwhelming. All feels well with the world for up to four hours, while users should still feel functional for most tasks. This mellow sativa buzz is nice for socializing and may have medicinal value for depression and obsessive thoughts or behaviors.

Dr. Greenthumb's Gallery

Dr. Greenthumb has been growing and breeding cannabis for over 25 years in Eastern Canada. He has strains for both indoor gardens and for outdoors in short-season climates. His seeds have been available since 1996. Check out his website: www.drgreenthumb.com for more info.

Endless Sky

Greenthumb Seeds

 90/10

 spacey/stoney

 earthy/hashy

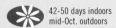 42-50 days indoors
mid-Oct. outdoors

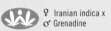 ♀ Iranian indica x
♂ Grenadine

 225 g (8 oz.) per plant

Dr. Greenthumb's breeding program emphasizes outdoor performance in Canada, and his Endless Sky strain is no exception, finishing by mid-October in its native latitudes. But Endless Sky is also a great indoor strain for growers seeking a potent, easily cultivated indica.

Like many indicas, Endless Sky does well in soil but really flourishes in hydro, where she grows very fast. Her moderate size and limited branching make Endless Sky a good choice for small spaces and sea of green gardens. When flowered at 10-12 inches tall, these plants reach 24-30 inches at harvest. If raised in a sea of green under a 400 watt HPS with an average 1500 parts per million of nutrient salts, Endless Sky will yield 400-500 grams (14-17 ounces) per square meter.

Endless Sky tends toward a single, tight and chunky central cola, although she may form a few short side branches. Buds range from soda-can size up to the size of two-liter soda bottle when ripe. The ripe buds are heavy for their girth and crusty with trichomes. Endless Sky's sun leaves are large and display characteristics midway between indicas and sativas, with a tendency toward the wider indica leaf pattern. Leaves often turn to pink or yellow-pink at maturity.

The poetic name is a pleasure to say but may also be a reflection on the buzz, which is very open and spacey. This variety produces a potent, indica-type stone that has been reported to provide pain relief. One hit warms your whole head almost instantly. This is not a good toke when preparing to drive or operate heavy machinery. Endless Sky's dense smoke tastes earthy, like hash, and produces a dreamy, hashy experience that lasts up to four hours.

The history of cannabis consumption stretches back at least four millennia, but the actual chemistry of the plant has only been unlocked in the last forty years.

The Plant Side: Cannabinoids

Marijuana is composed of over 400 compounds, including about 60 cannabinoids, which are a class of molecules unique to the cannabis plant. Cannabinoids were first identified in the 1940s, but it was not until 1964 that Dr. Raphael Mechoulam of the Hebrew University of Jerusalem isolated delta-9 tetrahydrocannabinol (THC), as the primary psychoactive ingredient in pot, the chemical that gets people high.

THC's effects are modulated by the other cannabinoids. Along with THC, the main cannabinoids are cannabidiol (CBD), cannabinol (CBN) and cannabigerol (CBG). More than 50 other cannabinoids are either slight chemical variations on these main four molecules, or are only present in extremely small quantities in comparison. THC is by far the best understood.

The molecular formula of THC is $C_{21}H_{30}O_2$, with a molecular weight of 314.45 and a boiling point of 200°C (392°F).

Cannabinoids are concentrated in a thick resin produced in glandular structures known as trichomes. This name comes from the Greek, and means "growth of hair." On marijuana plants, trichomes are the tiny stalks with cannabinoid-filled heads that stick up off the buds, leaves and stems. In addition to cananbinoids, trichomes are also rich in terpenes, the chemicals that produce the powerful, distinctive odors of the cannabis plant.

Photo: Tom Flowers

This close-up shows the glandular structure of marijuana resin. The ball atop the stem is the "trichome." It contains the cannabinoids, responsible for the high, and the terpenes, responsible for the odor and flavor of cannabis.

The Human Side: Cannabinoid Receptors

Cannabinoid receptors are found in very large quantities in many different parts of the nervous system, which includes the brain, spinal cord and the nerves that carry signals between the brain and body. Most of the cannabis high is the result of THC interacting with the cannabinoid receptors in the nervous system.

In 1988 an American research team discovered the part of the brain that picks up THC and other cannabinoids. Dubbed CB-1 receptors, they seem to be responsible for the euphoric and anticonvulsive effects of cannabis. CB-1 receptors are found in many parts of the nervous system and reproductive system, but are virtually absent from areas that control the lungs and heart. Marijuana bypasses these systems, making it essentially non-toxic. Most drugs, even aspirin or coffee, act on these vital systems, which means at high enough doses, they can be toxic or fatal to humans. On the contrary, there are no recorded deaths from a marijuana overdose. The effects of THC overconsumption are generally restricted to conditions that may include severe temporary memory impairment, paranoia and panic, but most often result in sleepiness followed by deep and sometimes prolonged sleep.

Scientists identified a second group of cannabis receptors known as CB-2 receptors. These are found in the immune system, primarily the spleen, but also in other organs. They appear to be responsible for the anti-inflammatory and stress reduction effects of marijuana. The CB-2 receptors may hold the key to many other therapeutic effects that this plant offers, such as immune modulation and tumor reduction.

Having identified these receptors, researchers naturally wondered what they were doing there in the first place. In 1992, Dr. Devane, along with a scientific team working at Dr. Mechoulam's project, was able to identify the chemical produced by the body naturally that the receptors are there to receive.

Devane named these naturally occuring chemicals "anandamides" after the Sanskrit word for bliss (ananda). Technically, they are described as "endogenous ligands." They activate the cannabinoid receptors. The effects of the natural chemicals are similar to THC, but act less powerfully and disappear far faster.

The discovery of these anandamides makes it clear that while cannabinoid receptors sure come in handy for getting high on pot, their sole purpose is not to allow humans to get high from cannabis. The cannabinoid system appears to be very ancient, and exists in nearly all species of animals so far investigated—mammals, reptiles and birds, even very simple ones like the microscopic hydra.

According to Mechoulam's ongoing research, anandamides may play a critical role in controlling many of the body's biochemical systems, including reproduction, sleep, fight-or-flight and appetite cycles. The presence of these naturally occurring "anandamides" gives new meaning to the saying "get high on life." Our bodies naturally take advantage of this feel-good chemistry for their own regulatory purposes.

Vaporizers are a healthier way to inhale.

Photo: Barge

The Cannabis-Human Interaction

Once THC reaches a cell, it binds to the receptor, causing changes in the cell's function, which ultimately result in the physiological or psychological effects of the drug—in other words, it makes you high.

The body absorbs pot when the cannabinoids are released and inhaled as smoke or vapor. They pass through the lining of the lungs and enter the bloodstream. Blood circulates through the heart, then heads straight for the brain and on to other parts of the body, resulting in a rapid onset of effects.

When cannabis is eaten or drunk as a beverage, the cannabinoids are not absorbed until they've made it past the stomach to the intestines, where they are absorbed into the blood, which passes through the liver before distribution to the brain and other parts of the body.

Photo: Barge

Once THC passes through the liver, it is chemically modified into 11-hydroxy-THC. Because digestion and absorption are relatively inefficient and slow, the effects are delayed for 30-60 minutes from consumption, but once they begin, they last longer.

The quality of the "high" from inhalation versus eating may be different, since most of the eaten THC will be modified by the liver. Also, only about 30% of the THC is absorbed when eaten, while 50-75% is absorbed when pot is inhaled, whether smoked or vaporized.

A scientific study of subjects smoking marijuana determined what factors affected blood levels of THC. It was discovered that longer breath holding time was more important than the number of puffs taken or the "puff volume." That's right. Roll your eyes at your smoking pals when they seem on the verge of exploding from holding an inhale—science is on their side.

Once pot reaches the receptors, it has a multitude of effects. Scientific researchers have indicated four main groups of psychological categories that make up the high[†]:

Emotional: euphoria, easy laughter, decreased anxiety
Sensory: increased or altered perception of external stimuli; increased awareness of one's own body

[†]Adapted from Perez-Reyes, M. "The psychologic and physiologic effects of active cannabinoids." In Nahas, G., et al, *Marijuana and Medicine*. Totowa, NJ; Humana Press, 1999, pp. 245-252.

Somatic: feeling of floating or sinking, impaired balance
Cognitive: distortion of time perception, memory lapses, difficulty concentrating

Physiological effects may include a brief increase in heart rate and blood pressure, red eyes, dry mouth, decreased activity of the intestines and decreased nausea, analgesia (pain relief), decreased convulsions (anti-seizure) and decreased muscle spasms. These effects may be present to greater or lesser degrees depending on the balance of cannabinoids and the amount of the dose.

The Science of Variety

Remember the two types of receptors? THC attaches primarily to CB-1 receptors, while CBD has an affinity for CB-2 receptors. Since some varieties have a larger proportion of CBD relative to THC or vice versa, this is one scientific basis for different strains producing a range of effects. More CBD typically produces a heavier, "body high," helpful with sleep or inflammation. More THC typically affects the head more, generating euphoria and energy.

Connoisseurs appreciate the subtleties of variation in the highs marijuana can impart. Now, the medical community is just beginning to identify physiologic reactions to certain strains that may benefit specific conditions. So far, it is believed that THC mediates pain and provides neuroprotection, while CBD relieves convulsion, inflammation, anxiety and nausea.

GW Pharmaceuticals, the British firm, has spent years and millions of dollars researching and developing cannabis-based medications. They have found that particular balances of these two cannabinoids produce measurably different effects in patients. For instance, THC or CBD alone do not help pain management nearly as much as an equal balance between the two.

Other cannabinoids also appear to have profound effects on physical function and health. Since 2002, cancer researchers have identified cannabinoids responsible for tumor reduction, triggering the natural cell death that keeps tumors from growing and cutting off the blood supply to tumors that have already developed.

Identifying and developing strains of marijuana that contain particular ratios of cannabinoids and other chemicals should prove to be some of the most important work of the next decade.

Photo: Chad Man

Ethiopian Highland

African Seeds

Africa Seeds obtained the original seed stock for Ethiopian Highland from the breeders in the Rasta community in Shashemene, a sprawling town located in the Great Rift Valley, about 150 miles from Ethiopia's capital Addis Ababa. The strain originated in the Highland region of southern Tanzania, and then was brought to Ethiopia where it was grown for many generations before reaching African Seeds breeders.

This pure sativa has never been crossed, only inbred. Outdoors, Ethiopian thrives when grown in a location with a long warm summer, but it will also do well at northern European latitudes and cooler high altitude mountain climates. This plant can also be tamed for indoor gardens as long as the lighting is fairly intense. Ebb and flow hydro is a better choice of systems; this plant is difficult to grow in soil indoors.

African Seeds typically allows this heavily branched, shorter sativa strain to grow vegetatively outdoors for 12-16 weeks before flowering. In cooler climates with long summer daylight hours, 8-10 weeks of vegetative cycle is sufficient. Of course yield is partly dependent on how big the plants are allowed to get before they are flowered. Indoors, this strain should veg for at least 6 weeks before flowering is forced. Once forced to flower, ripening only takes about a month.

Ethiopian Highland buds are loose, long and fluffy, tucked between the slender, light green foliage. When smoked, it has a very strong, burley Turkish aroma with a licorice aftertaste. The buzz is electric and energetic, good for recreation or daytime use because mental clarity is intact and the potential for couchlock is low. This strain is used by the local Rasta community and others in Ethiopia for religious and medicinal uses.

clear, electric

tobacco, licorice

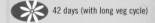
42 days (with long veg cycle)

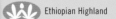
Ethiopian Highland

2-4 oz. indoors
10-20 oz. outoors

Seeds of Passion

Dutch Passion started as a cannabis seed company in 1987 in Amsterdam, producing premium quality cannabis seeds in the Netherlands. Known for their sophistication and quality, Dutch Passion is a company with a love for the science of breeding. From development to delivery, Dutch Passion breeders concerned themselves with creating and preserving quality. Their varieties back up their reputation, with multiple prizes in cup competitions.

One of this company's passions has been revolutionizing the feminization of seeds. Five years ago, Dutch Passion released a line of feminized seeds and now offers 25 such strains along with their 30 varieties of regular seeds.

Scientific consideration has also gone into their packaging, which is professionally sealed to maintain germination rates. Dutch Passion has also been busy reaching out to its customers. The fruits of their labor are available in over 450 grow shops, head shops and web sites, of course mainly focused in Europe. Their two retail Seeds of Passion Global Seed Shops are located in Holland, one in Maastricht and one in Amsterdam, and boast an extensive offering of 200 varieties from 20 well-established seed companies from South Africa, Canada, Switzerland, Spain, England and Holland.

The Seeds of Passion Store in Amsterdam

The Amsterdam shop can be found a short walk away from the Rembrandtsplein, at Utrechtstraat 26. This lovely little boutique is identifiable by the huge sprouting seed that is Dutch Passion's logo. Outside of Amsterdam, information about their company, including their feminized line, is available through their web sites:

www.dutch-passion.nl
www.seedsofpassion.nl

Euforia

Dutch Passion

In Greek, "euphoria" means "having health," as in physical health or an intense feeling of well-being. Fittingly, Dutch Passion's Euforia is a very healthy, disease-resistant plant. She grows strong with minimal tending indoors or out, and flourishes in Southern Europe and similar climates. She also of course provides the euphoric bliss that smokers want from primo cannabis.

Indoors, Euforia is a performer that delivers on any stage, whether grown in soil, coco, or hydro, as a multi-branch or in a sea of green. She is a "half open" plant with widely spaced foliage, not bushy, and usually does not need branch supports even though her buds can get quite hefty. Because her branching and foliage is minimal, Euforia requires only the lightest of pruning for maximizing light and harvest. Careful growers start removing fan leaves slowly in week eight of flowering. She will stay strictly green unless she is grown outside, in which case her medium-thick leaves may range into purple tones.

Indoors, this variety reaches 80-100 cm (32-40 inches) in 30 days on average, and can be harvested after 9 weeks, the end of her second flowering wave. Some people like to wait for a bumper harvest that will come about a month after initial harvest; in other words, Euforia flowers three times and yields twice over 13-14 weeks in total.

This sweet, blossom-scented variety delivers a very pleasing and up high. It is an active pot, which can be useful medicinally when marijuana's soothing properties need to be balanced with lucidity and energy. Euforia also adds a smile to the recreational smoker's day without hampering other activities if used in moderation. However it is less desirable as a before bed toke, and may even keep smokers awake. Euforia has won awards at the *High Times* Cannabis Cup and the High Life Cup.

 80/20

 up, active

 floral

 63 days indoors
end Oct. outdoors

 ♀ part Skunk x
♂ part Skunk

 25-30 g (1 oz.) per plant
indoors (SOG)
200-250 g (7-9 oz.) outdoors

 SOG

Exile

Magus Genetics

 70/30

 narcotic, sleepy

 fresh, pine

 60-67 days

 ♀ White Widow 25% x
♀ Northern Lights 25% x
♂ Warlock 50%

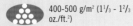 400-500 g/m² (1¹/₃ - 1²/₃ oz./ft.²)

 SOG

Magus Genetics likes to give its strains romantic names. In this case, the Exile is not a punishment, but more of an escape from circling thoughts and worries, a little mental vacation. The word "Exile" also sounds strong and isolated, which reflects this strain's singularly deep, powerful indica stone.

Exile is adaptable enough to grow well in any of the usual indoor setups. To a certain extent growers can control Exile's branching to suit their cultivation style. Exile's nodes develop at right angles to the stalk, proliferating medium branches on top of each other. This is true both of mature plants and cuttings, and especially likely in low to medium intensity light. Thus growers can alter Exile's branching pattern by adjusting her light intensity. If a gardener wants columnar plants for a sea of green, the vegetative period should be shorter and the light should be kept more intense. Weaker lights on the other hand will encourage multiple branching.

Exile's multiple branches sprout more large, dark green leaves than its parent strains. Its pistils are cream coloured changing to tan with maturity. As it flowers, Exile's foliage exudes a jolting sweet pine scent that gets much tamer in the dried buds, giving the smoke a soft pine needle flavor.

Exile is a very narcotic body stone. It is the main course, a smoke for people who don't have anything planned for a few hours besides dreaming. Magus Genetics is properly cautious about making medical claims. Like alcohol, Exile's indica knockout helps some users sleep but can backfire as a treatment for chronic insomnia. There are also reports of relief from multiple sclerosis symptoms.

G-13 Haze x NYC Diesel
Soma Seeds

The G-13 Haze x New York City Diesel is one of several G-13 crosses that Soma has developed from his signature strains. This pleasure pot has an exotic combination that evokes the aroma of old-school Thai-stick and the red grapefruit taste of the NYC Diesel.

This strain is an indoor plant in most locales, and is only suitable outdoors in tropical settings. The G-13 Haze/Diesel is happy in soil or a hydroponics setup, as long as it is allowed to branch out. It does especially well when super-cropped, producing plump, fairly dense flowers at close internodes. The main stalk is very strong and sturdy. Until the last three weeks, this plant stays green, but in the last phases of flowering, it may acquire a lavender hue on the bud and foliage.

The high from G-13 Haze x NYC Diesel is truly joyous. Its mood elevating qualities often creep up, shifting perspective to clear, light and happy thoughts. It encourages a sense of connectedness and may send the smoker on a hugging binge, or at least a sweet and gentle attitude toward friends and the world at large. Best indulged when one's environment supports a loving demeanor, this strain is also potentially helpful for depression. The smell and taste have retained grapefruit tones from the Diesel, but the uniquely Haze aroma comes through in the smoke. Opening a container of cured buds releases a smell like a case of ripe fruit.

 60/40

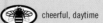 cheerful, daytime

 Thai stick, red grapefruit

 70-90 days indoors
end Oct.-end Nov. outdoors

 ♂ G-13 Haze x
♀ NYC Diesel

 40-60 g (1³/₄-2¹/₂ oz.)
per plant

Soma on the G-13 Haze

G-13 is a strain of mythical proportions, the stuff of urban legends. Bred in Kentucky, G-13 was developed by a U.S. government research program. It found its way to Holland and the talented hands of the breeder Nevil in the early 1980s. He was one of the first cannabis seed producers in the Netherlands. In 1988 he made the G-13/Haze cross, and I managed to get my hands on ten of the seeds germinated from this cross. Only one of my seeds delivered, but it was a male. My only choice was to cross the G-13/Haze to my existing strains.

I believe these crosses are my finest work to date. I have made eleven separate crosses, and they all have a little something extra to offer thanks to the influence of the G-13-Haze. The strains range in their sativa/indica profile, with most nearly equal in genotype. They all carry through some of the sativa qualities in the high, although the other characteristics range from very abstract and cerebral to giggly to catlike laziness. Whichever strain is chosen from the G-13/Haze collection, it offers something positive in the healing arts, which benefits all whether the intent is specifically medicinal or not.

Soma Seeds varieties crossed with G-13/Haze: Buddha's Sister, Somango, Somativa, White Willow, Lavender, Citralah, White Light, NYC Diesel, Rockbud, Reclining Buddha, Free Tibet.

Photo: Soma

God's Treat

Jordan of the Islands

Cannabis is considered a sacred plant in some circles. God's Treat is a name that is both promising and slightly whimsical. The name actually takes one word each from its parents, Dutch Treat and God Bud, both dark green, strong indicas with a reputation for powerful flavor and fun highs. This resilient variety is a determined grower that thrives indoors and outdoors in most climates.

God's Treat, like its parents, is quite branchy and does best when this growth is controlled but encouraged in multi-branch cultivation, rather than trimmed for the sea of green type single-cola method. Her flowering time is a highly desirable 6-7 weeks. By harvest time these plants are still quite short and bush-like with fat, football-shaped buds. The slightly loose, airy structure of the flowers gives them better resistance to molds or other nuisances of wet climates. Although the plant's overall structure has indica tendencies, the leaves are light green and thin, more sativa-like in profile than either parent.

At harvest, God's Treat gleams with tantalizing crystals. Her aroma and flavor fuse herbal and candy into a sweet alloy that's hard to describe. Her stone adds sativa's blissful head-chakra uplift to the sensuality and durability of indica. God's Treat offers a lasting high that envelops the mind and body in a lighthearted, spiritually elevated flight.

  75/25

 uplifting, mellow, longlasting

 floral candy

 42-50 days

 ♀ Dutch Treat x ♂ God Bud

 4-8 oz. per plant indoors
8-12 oz. per plant outdoors

Hawaiian Snow

Greenhouse Seed Co.

In the commercial seed world, this strain is as rare as snow in Hawaii—a long season equatorial with a triple-haze parentage. Hazes are popular for their light fresh taste and radiant highs, but they require more care and patience than the usual fare of commercially available strains.

Hawaiian Snow's lengthy ripening time confines her indoors except in the most favorable climates. Large and rangy, she should be grown under 18 hours of light for a short vegetative period. Hawaiian Snow's size and slow flowering make her unsuitable for sea of green setups. This variety needs a big pot of soil with a low acid content (starting at a pH of 6.0). Flowering takes at least 14 weeks. Growers can smoke their faster strains while anticipating Snow's payoff – the mental dawn that only comes from slow-ripening hazes.

Hawaiian Snow grows in a pine-tree profile, with wide distances between internodes. Topping her elongated branches is counterproductive while bending achieves amazing results. The slender leaves will be bright green, darkening during flowering, then lightening as the plants are flushed for harvest. Buds are long and compact with big calyxes, profuse hairs and a lovely sugar coating of resin.

Hawaiian Snow's rich spicy sativa taste leaves some mint freshness behind on exhale. Its complex mix of aromas and flavors evokes eucalyptus, lemon grass and a hint of musk and green moss. As the flavor fades, the high reveals itself: the body stays alert while the moods and thoughts enter a space of elation, which encourages freethinking and a sense of wellbeing. It is a lovely social high that lowers tensions and incites laughter.

Hawaiian Snow won 1st prize (overall) at the 2003 *High Times* Cannabis Cup.

 90/10

 creative, cerebral, creeper

 herbal fresh and minty

 105-112 days indoors

 ♀ Hawaiian Haze x
♀ Pure Haze x
♂ Neville's Haze

 100 to 120 grams (3-4 oz.) per plant (5 gal. pots)

Heavy Duty Fruity

T.H. Seeds

 60/40

 sleepy, couch lock, munchies

 deep fruit, nutty edge

 60-63 days indoors
mid to end Oct. outdoors

 ♀ Killing Garberville x
♂ Seattle Big Bud x
♂ Mendocino Hash Plant

 1 g per watt

 when topped

Heavy Duty Fruity has a major kick, whether your shtick is yield, flavor or stoniness. A nearly even mix of sativa and indica, this plant derives its heritage from the U.S. West Coast marijuana belt, mixing strains from Northern California's sweet spots with a daddy from the more temperate and wet Pacific Northwest. T.H. Seeds thanks Medicine Man for introducing this strain to them.

Heavy Duty Fruity can be grown indoors or out, but is especially recommended for the hydroponics gardener. This heavy-weight performer's strong fruity dankness will fill the grow room—and the surrounding areas if odor is not controlled. The buds reach monstrous sizes on a steady diet of high EC nutrients. Excellent yields can also be expected from outdoor plants, which will be ready in the last half of October when grown at Holland's latitude.

This variety is great as a multi-topped plant, with many sites for its dense and hefty buds. The leaves are not always the classic seven-pointers. They're often thick and gnarly, and some eventually change color from green to purple.

Heavy Duty Fruity's pungent fruit odor penetrates the air and fills the senses, making ozone generators or another air cleaning method essential where inconspicuousness is key. The stone is dependent on harvesting time. If a psychedelic couchlock buzz is preferred, then harvesting at the earliest phase of ripeness, usually about 50-60 days, is recommended. However, for a mellower, sleepier goodnight stone, growers mature the harvest for a full nine weeks. Munchies are another quality that may come on heavy duty, which makes this a good medical treatment for appetite loss.

Jack Flash

Sensi Seed Bank

The Jack Herer strain—named for the outstanding hemp activist—is an esteemed prizewinner, but its complex genetics and Haze tendencies require experienced, patient gardening for good results. Jack Flash derives from Jack Herer genetics, retaining many of its desirable characteristics while improving its ease and success in the garden.

Jack Flash will gratify the indoor gardener with its vigor, ease and performance. It can be grown in any medium and as a single or multiple branch plant. Its tendency is to grow tall and narrow, forming one central cola. Given this predisposition, Jack Flash needs less floor space than many indicas require.

Jack Flash's leaves reflect its sativa ancestry—they are light green in tone with long, narrow blades. The buds display more of an indica growth pattern, forming big solid clumps around the internodes; however, there will be some sativa 'run' as the buds mature and spread along the branches. By harvest, there are almost no gaps in the top 1/3 of the plant. Jack Flash buds produce the rotund, resin-coated, calyxes prized by growers. This phenotype can be spotted early in flowering from its very dense, almost angular bud formation, displaying extremely short pairs of hairs. In the last four weeks, these clusters begin to run along the branches, swelling as if inflated with a bike pump.

The Jack Flash aroma is fruity like Jack Herer, but with a little more skunkiness. The smoke tastes acrid, with a hint of sweetness in the aftertaste. This Jack gets to work in a flash, reverberating through one's head like a bell on the first few tokes. This immediate zing quickly segues into a warm sociable high, good for chilling and chatting at your favorite coffee shop or other watering hole.

Jack Flash won the Dutch High Life Cup (overall) in 1998.

 I S 55/45

 relaxing, then warm and cerebral

 acrid, fruity with hint of pungency

 50 – 70 days

 ♀ Northern Lights #5 x
♀ SKC1-Rood x
♂ SK 1 8.5 F3A

 125 g (4 1/2 oz.) per plant

 SOG

69

Kalichakra

Mandala Seeds

Kalichakra was named after the Hindu Godess Kali, the consort to the ganja smoking Lord Shiva famed for her omnipotent powers over life and death. This sativa prefers a warm, sunny climate when grown outdoors, but can also tolerate harsh weather due to her robust nature and resistance to mold. Kalichakra gives best results indoors when a minimum of 600 watts per square meter of light is provided. She also tolerates temperatures above the ideal.

Hydro and soil are equally good methods for this variety, but height must be monitored in a hydroponic system. Kalichakra, like many sativas, grows tall and will shoot up in a tremendously short time. The side shoots that develop at the internodes are vigorous, arching upward with little branching in between. Kalichakra's quality branch development make her an excellent candidate for motherhood.

When allowed to grow naturally, Kalichakra is a resinous, high yielding plant that disperses buds on all branches rather than concentrating flowering potential in one central cola. Her space conscious growth pattern allows her to be planted in close rows to maximize yield even in smaller spaces. Buds vary in shape: some are compact spheres, others are more stretched and airy.

Kalichakra has a potent and energizing body effect that awakens the Kundalini—the divine life-energy coiled like a snake at the base of the spine. It is a refreshing, strong stone for creative activities or social interaction. When indulged in heavily, this variety may cause a temporary bliss-out.

This strain has been used successfully for pain relief, and against depression. It is recommended for those seeking a long lasting high. Kalichakra exhumes a distinct spicy-fresh, herblike aroma when you rub the stems and flowers. The dried buds retain most of these aromatic qualities but are mild in taste and pleasantly smooth to smoke.

alert, psychedelic

mild spicy/fresh

70-75 days indoors
end Oct. outdoors

♀ Crystal Queen x
♂ White Satin

500-600 g/m² (1½ -
2 oz./ft.²) dry weight

71

Kariba Surprise

African Seeds

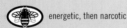
energetic, then narcotic

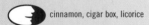
cinnamon, cigar box, licorice

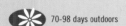
70-98 days outdoors

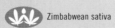
Zimbabwean sativa

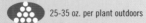
25-35 oz. per plant outdoors

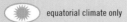
equatorial climate only

Among the Batonka people of Southern Africa, aristocratic wives could once be seen chatting and puffing away on ornate mahogany pipes filled with *dagga* (cannabis). While their homeland was destroyed in 1958 with the construction of a massive artificial lake at Kariba, Zimbabwe, a few pockets of traditional Batonka life – and dagga cultivation – can be found in the remote Chizarira National Park, where the tribe has relocated. The Kariba Surprise strain shares some general qualities with African sativas while capturing the unique genetics of a near-vanished tribe of pot agronomists.

Kariba Surprise is pure unhybridized sativa—a tall, heavily branched plant that forms fluffy loose buds with long red and white hairs. Grown in their hot native environment, this mold-resistant plant ranges between 9 and 14 feet in height with buds of lengths up to 2 feet long. The fan leaves get huge but stay thin and gain a darker green than most sativas. These plants can be finished with a full cycle of 16-20 weeks of good outdoor climate.

On ripening, Kariba Surprise is potent with THC, and almost entirely lacking in CBD. The Batonka used this strain recreationally as well as for pain control and religious rituals. Initially, smoking Kariba will bring a surge of energy, but this fades gradually into a more narcotic, sedating effect. The high is longlasting and great for a personal day or times when engaging creative pursuits. The aroma is in the range typical of African sativas—a complex earthy spice that suggests mocha java coffee, cinnamon, tobacco and licorice.

KC #39

KC Brains

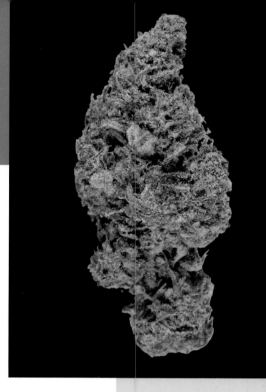

Back in 1974, some globetrotting Dutch hippies were returning to Europe from the newly accessible Hindu Kush region. During their adventures, they'd acquired some seeds, which they'd brought back and handed off to a grower in Spain. The Spanish grower maintained this indica variety over the years. More than twenty years had passed since this strain made its journey west when KC happened to meet the Spanish grower in a Dutch coffeeshop. KC got some of these Spain-acclimated Kush seeds, which he then crossed with KC 606, a very indica-strong standard from his seed library. The resulting cross is KC #39, a strong indica with dark leaves and a dark, slightly spicy aroma.

This variety flowers very early, and is great for outdoor growing in Amsterdam's latitude or other temperate regions. Because her compact buds resist mold, KC #39 will tolerate environments with moderate humidity or notable rainfall. This plant will finish by the end of September when flowering is started in July. The buds retain light green tones during flowering while the extra-wide leaves turn an inky-dark jade.

The KC #39 buzz is very, very stoney in a physical sense, and may profoundly warp reality at its peak. After the initial cliff drop into the stone, it is possible to follow the thread of conversation although many will find they are happier listening than speaking – conversationalists in this relaxed state can catch the mumbles. KC #39 encourages spectatorship more than interaction on most levels, except possibly where snacking is involved. Others will simply find that this is a potent tonic for inviting sleep.

I

stoney

dark & pungent

49-63 days indoors
end Sept. outdoors

♀ indica seeds from
Spanish friend (1996) x
♂ KC 606 (1999)

200 g (7 oz.) per plant
indoors
1 kilo (2 lbs.) per plant
outdoors

KC #42

KC Brains

This strain derives from what some claim is New Zealand's primo pot. KC got the New Zealand seeds in 1999 from a gal traveler who brought them back to Amsterdam where she worked in a coffeeshop. He hybridized this strain with a very hazey, part-Brazilian male, the KC 639, to arrive at KC #42, a haze-like sativa with a fresh lemony-grassy taste.

KC #42 is a good add-on strain for an intermediate or pro cultivator. It is less appropriate for beginners. This strain has high standards of cleanliness and shows her displeasure when gardening standards are lax.

Indoors, KC #42 grows in soil or hydro. She can be placed directly into a flowering light cycle from a rooted clone. This girl likes to bush out —supportive netting allows her many branches to rest and be arranged to some degree, maximizing the light that reaches her flowering sites. Although KC #42 can be grown in the great outdoors, she won't finish until the end of November or beginning of December – frost season in most parts of the world.

The buds of KC #42 are wooly tufts that spread along her many branches. Although not hidden by much leaf production, these sprawling buds still take extra time to manicure. The effort pays off, though, with a basket of fluffy green sativa popcorn harvested from all over the plant.

This is a serious kick-back sativa. The stone is good fuel for mental wandering and late-night poetic-philosophical jam sessions. Unlikely to set the mood for a late night out dancing on the town, KC #42 suits a night when relaxation and the comforts of home are on the menu.

hazy, couch lock, wandering mind

lemon & haze

63-84 days

♀ New Zealand Best (1999) x ♂ KC 639 (2001)

150 g (5 oz.) per plant

Kerala Krush

Flying Dutchmen

Photo: Cannabis College

Kerala, the Southern tip of the Indian subcontinent, is famous for goddess-centered Hinduism, tropical forests, white beaches, and blasting cannabis highs. Kerala Krush is an extremely vigorous hybrid—the result of pure Keralan sativa crossed with the robust Skunk #1. This sativa hybrid offers a Zen high, good yields and reasonable maturation times.

Kerala Krush can be grown indoors, or outdoors from 45 degrees latitude right down to the equator. A greenhouse is a great compromise for outdoor gardeners in temperate regions. Flying Dutchmen recommends growing this variety organically in soil, but all other growing methods are suitable.

A slender plant of medium height, Kerala Krush has narrow leaflets and long petioles. Indoors, best results are attained through pruning once or twice before flowering. Bending the lateral branches to 45 degrees reduces stretching by allowing light to distribute evenly throughout all the budding sites. Individual bracts are large and very resinous when left to mature fully. Buds form into long slender sativa-type flowers. Toward the end of the flowering cycle, the buds swell and become heavy and dense—the slight indica influence of Skunk #1. Maturation times indoors are between 9 and 11 weeks with a 12/12 photoperiod.

Outdoors at 45 degrees latitude Kerala Krush matures in the first half of November, earlier if closer to the equator. A full May-November season outdoors produces plants over 3 meters (9 feet) tall when left unpruned. A good climate gives yields in excess of 500 grams per plant. The buds keep their weight and structure well when carefully dried and cured.

Kerala Krush has an extremely clear, cerebral high—potent and smooth from start to finish. Her palate mixes cool fruit and warm spice. Medicinally sativa strains may be appropriate for appetite stimulation, menstrual cramps and controlling chemotherapy nausea.

 87.5/12.5

 clear-headed, cerebral

 sweet mango/spice

 63-77 days indoors
mid-Nov. outdoors

 ♀ South Indian (P1) x
♂ Original Skunk #1 (P1)

 0.75 g per watt of light

 SOG

75

The Males

It is in breeding that males tranform from a nuisance to a necessity in the garden. But how do you choose a male to father great daughters? That is the marijuana breeder's dilemma.

A breeder male should be vigorous, healthy and resistant to problems that plague lesser males. It should ripen at the time the breeder wants, and it should lend qualities that complement its mate. Better yet if the male selected for breeding has a little something special going on. Perhaps it is more pungent, or has more glands than its buddies. Here are a few that made the cut.

G-13 Haze male Photo: Soma

Early Swazi male Photo: Greenthumb Seeds, Canada

Young Male Flower

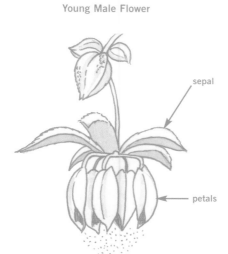

sepal

petals

The flower most clearly identifies
the male plant.

Male branches and pre-flowers are
only subtly different from the female.

Warlock male Photo: Magus Genetics

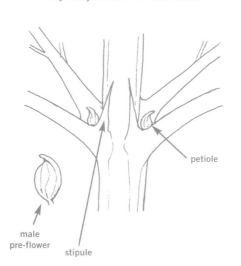

petiole

male
pre-flower

stipule

Ilustrations: K. Abellán

77

Lethal Purple

Great White North

Growers who like to see purple will be thrilled by this strain's color. While some varieties become tinged with purple, especially when the temperatures drop, the Lethal Purple strain turns entirely purple by the time it reaches ripeness. Developed by a company whose specialty is outdoor strains for temperate climes, Lethal Purple delivers happy smoke in a gracefully short growing season.

This sativa–dominant strain was developed to be grown in the great outdoors. On the prairies of Canada, Lethal Purple finishes at the end of September, reaching a height between 5 and 6½ feet. The many branches sport long foxtail bud formations that are loose and airy with a detectable floral perfume.

In Canada, the average yield per plant is 4 ounces, but at lower latitudes where the fall season is long, yields can reach 12 or more ounces on each plant if the grower provides proper fertilization. Lethal Purple's high is excellent, with a smooth entry into the sensation, and a light yet potent mental exhilaration that raises the mood while remaining functional.

 60/40

 happy, functional

 perfume, flowers

 end Sept.

 purple strains

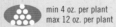 min 4 oz. per plant
max 12 oz. per plant

Lionheart

Almighty Seeds

Lionheart started with a surprise cross between African and U.S. genetics, which resulted in a plant that outperformed its garden mates by leaps and bounds. The breeder found the potency and the duration of the high to be superior to the other strains in development.

Best grown in pots or in a bucket setup, Lionheart is a natural multi-brancher intended for the outdoors even in northern climates like Canada. She requires little beyond basic care, and will outgrow any outdoor pests or competing bushes. She puts out long branches everywhere, each branch resembling a new plant. By harvest time there are worthy colas even at lower parts of the plant that get little light. Optimal yields can be obtained by spreading out her viney branches on a trellis. Lionheart's roots grow extremely fast, although this plant's cuttings are difficult to root. Buds are numerous, not rock hard but heavy, mold resistant and highly resinous. Her fan leaves turn yellow in fall, allowing more light into the canopy and making manicuring easy.

When cured, Lionheart takes on a reddish brown color and has an incredibly long shelf life. Even buds that have been put aside in a box will stay sticky to the touch, breaking down into smaller nuggets rather than crumbling into dust. When fresh buds are crushed, fingers are left extremely sticky and the bud forms tight, stubborn little nuggets. The aroma resembles incense with a minimal green plant smell, and often overtakes the aroma of other strains in the room. When smoked as a pure joint or in a pipe, the buds burn very thick and slow, refusing to extinguish even when not being puffed. Spicy, appealing and intense, this high is a quality sativa, edifying to the mind and celebratory. This strain stands up to the test of time, continuing to deliver a good stone even with long-term regular use.

 S

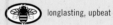 longlasting, upbeat

 intense spicy

 mid-late Sept.

 African sativa x U.S. #14 sativa

 varies

79

Lowryder

Joint Doctor's High-Bred Seeds

 I S

 creeper, uplifting

 mild with earthy overtones

 40-45 days indoors
60 days after seed is sown
outdoors

 ♀ Original William's Wonder
x ♂ Northern Lights #2
(Oasis) crossed with
Ruderalis-like variety

 14-45 g (¹/₂ - 2 oz.)
per plant

 SOG

A bonsai in the marijuana kingdom, Lowryder is a hybrid that was inbred and selected for nine generations, resulting in an extremely versatile plant that progresses from seed to bud in a mere two months.

Lowryder plants stay almost comically small, growing no taller than 16 inches, while 12 inches is typical. All plants autoflower in a short period of time. After a 2-3 week seedling phase, these plants go directly into flowering and finish in a speedy 40-45 days. Indoors, Lowryder performs well in soil or hydro systems, especially in sea of green setups. Due to the autoflowering characteristic, lights can be left on for 18 or 24 hours a day, while a 12/12 cycle only diminishes growth and yields. Because Lowryder's life cycle is short, cloning is often impractical.

Outdoors, Lowryder can be grown in virtually any climate, and has pushed the envelope with successful cultivation in unlikely places such as Finland, the Northwest Territories and other high latitude or altitude locations with very short seasons. Due to the diminutive size, this strain is also well adapted and easily concealed when cultivated in a backyard or patio garden, or as a windowsill plant.

Lowryder forms one main bud that averages 6 inches in length. Smaller buds start very close to the ground, and form along other branches, exhibiting very close nodes. They have a slightly irregular shape with thick pistils and orange coloration. This strain's leaf blades are often slightly whorled with long petioles, which give ample clearance between the stem and leaf for bud formation and air circulation on this pint-sized plant.

The Lowryder high comes on slowly, uplifting with its smooth yet strong smoke that tastes of pleasant, earthy undertones. This is a well-rounded buzz that is suited for outdoor activities.

The Lowryder Odyssey

Aptly named for its low profile in both a literal and figurative sense, the Lowryder strain was developed by the Joint Doctor in a ten-year mission for a "dwarf" marijuana variety.

In a veritable "weed odyssey" that began in his teens, Joint Doctor sought out old and new cannabis landraces and varieties, cultivation techniques, research methods and cultural practices. His travels and discoveries convinced Joint Doctor that nearly anything is possible in marijuana breeding. Even so, the idea of a bonsai strain would take a few years to form.

One summer while in Eastern Europe, Joint Doctor was visiting a friend whose family lived in a typically small cramped working-class apartment. The summer before, he'd given seeds to this pot-friendly family, which they planned to grow on their windowsill. Although he doubted this was practical, it led the Joint Doctor to conjecture: "Wouldn't that be neat if someone could develop a dwarf type of pot that was meant strictly for windowsills, balconies and cramped apartments?" He began searching for ways to breed smaller cannabis that would suit confined spaces, both indoor and out.

Much trial and error later, Lowryder was created. Lowryder grows from seed to bud in a fast 8 weeks. Its unique size and versatility combine with its short cycle to make it an easily concealed plant, whether in gardens or on patios and windowsills. It can be harvested several times per season without attracting undue attention, and has been grown everywhere from urban apartment balconies to arctic tundra. "From guerilla-style bush patches to urban basements to suburban backyards—even the skylight of a camper van, I have tried it all," Joint Doctor says.

The original Williams Wonder is crossed with a Northern Lights #2 indica and a mystery strain that carried an autoflowering trait. One drawback: Lowryder is difficult to clone or regenerate. Lowryder works best when successive crops are replanted from seed. Joint Doctor says that this variety is 100% stable, reliable in its properties and hermaphrodite-free. The high is potent and the resin production is quality. Lowryder's unique genetic and practical advantages give it an important niche in the world of fine cannabis, as well as the medical user's backyard pharmacopoeia.

Magic Bud

Paradise Seeds

Magic Bud offers growers fast, easy cultivation and a balance of indica and sativa traits. Sativa strains generally produce an energetic cerebral high – thoughts speed up but also become more flexible, happier, less mired in habit and fear. Indica stones often relax the body and amplify the senses, sometimes awakening the body's natural appetites. The sought-after combination stone offered by this mixed strain is a good mental and physical lubricant for social or creative challenges.

Magic Bud is a medium-sized plant with green velvet foliage. She grows a bit bushy and yields to her best potential when given space to branch. This variety ripens her magical flowers in only fifty days indoors, or mid-October outdoors in Holland. At maturity her branch tips swell with beautiful and aromatic resin-coated nugs. Her sweet taste along with her fast yield and balanced stone can make Magic Bud a good staple strain for all kinds of growers.

Magic Bud produces a very sweet flower with a spice bouquet, which can tempt growers to snip off some of her yield prematurely. While mouth-watering, her odor is strong, and may require some masking. Once cured and dried, Magic Bud tastes sweet and is easy on the lungs and the mind, leaving behind the potent magical ease, that desired quality of a pleasing smoke when a creative and positive mental high is the desired effect.

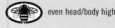 even head/body high

 floral

 50 days indoors
mid-Oct. at 50 degrees N

 sativa and indica strains

 400 g/m² indoors
500 g(17 oz.) per plant
outdoors

 out between 15-50°
latitude N and S

Manitoba Poison

Great White North

Manitoba Poison is a knockout stone for the great outdoor grower: a fast relaxation and sleeping agent that combines African strains for hardy growth and an early finish outdoors on Canada's prairies. Prospects for growing this plant outdoors at other latitudes are good, but it is especially useful in climates with short 6-7 week growing seasons and long days over summer. While Manitoba Poison works well as a multi-branch, the breeders prefer to pack them tightly in an outdoor sea of green.

This variety grows to about 4 feet (130 centimeters) tall. Her thick and durable jade leaves often darken to purple tones as she ripens. Manitoba Poison's buds also take on purple coloration, and form dense, very mold-resistant balls or ovals. The short season and hardy flowering are reasons why this plant thrives in the temperate northern climates of Canada, the northern U.S., or Europe, ripening as early as September at 50 degrees North latitude. Manitoba Poison grows a central cola and large branches with tops that cluster heavily with bud. When well manicured, her flowers look as if they were grown indoors. On the whole, this is a very easy strain to flower and tend. Manitoba Poison has a fresh, woodsy flavor and is essentially body relaxing and drowsy in its stone.

 50/50

 quick onset, sleepy

 fresh, woodsy

 beg. Sept.

 unnamed African strains

 115-230g (4-8 oz.) per plant

SOG

Maple Leaf Indica

Sensi Seed Bank

This pure indica strain grows dark, fat leaves that suggest both the classic "marijuana" symbol and the maple leaf symbol of Canada. This variety is a potent pure indica with an expansive sweetness that is pleasantly free of acridity, even in its largest colas.

Maple Leaf's "hero" buds develop along the main stem. When growing big plants, she can be topped to form a multi-branching plant with good results. When growing smaller or in sea of green, these plants cooperate nicely, producing little side branching which allows for good yields and minimal pruning in the space available. The internodes are close, even when plants are grown to bigger sizes. Maple Leaf Indica creates a lovely gloss of resin coating to protect its precious flowers from the elements. The glands stay slick and clear right up to harvest, rather than turning milky and opaque, which is generally an indication of a thicker cellulose capsule on the gland rather than greater cannabinoid content. The buds usually have rounded indica tops, ending in a cluster of three or more ovaries, rather than a single "point."

Once it is properly cured and dried, Maple Leaf Indica stash retains a sweet, somewhat incense-like palate from her Afghan parentage, with no hints of the less favorable odors of the pot palate. So long as it is not overindulged to the point of sleepiness, this variety is purported to have aphrodisiac properties. It provides a warm body hum that relaxes and enhances physical sensations, helping set an inviting mood for romance, dining or the appreciation of music or a good movie.

 sensual body stone

 sweet, sandalwood

 45-50 days indoors

 ♀ Ort 15 x Sam crossed with Afghan Skunk x ♂ Skunk 18.5

 up to 120g (4¼ oz.) per plant

 out between 40° latitude N and S

 SOG

Marley's Collie

Sensi Seed Bank

"Collie" was the standard slang-word for cannabis in Kingston, Jamaica, during Bob Marley's youth. Impressed by meeting Rita Marley at a cannabis event, Sensi Seeds breeders crossed some great Jamaican collie with a Maple Leaf relative as a tribute to the Marley family. "Marley" is a big name to live up to in the ganja world, but this indica-sativa cross has so far earned a lot of community good-will, winning the Dutch High Life Cup – the overall High Life prize – in 1999.

Marley's Collie can be grown outdoors in climates within 40 degrees latitude of the equator, but it is usually raised indoors in Holland. She reaches 130-160 centimeters if vegetated for 3-4 weeks. Her huge central bud and light, tractable branching make her ideal for sea of green growing – or she can be encouraged to spread out in a greenhouse. Soil and hydro are equally good growing media. Sensi advises growers not to top the central stem (unless their phenotype has proven to like topping), as Marley's Collie will often cease to grow a main stem (instead of splitting into two) and concentrate its energies on the surrounding branches. This tends to lower her yield.

This strain's buds are syrupy, with hairs visibly protruding in distinct pairs from each ovary. These pistils give her buds a 'spiky' appearance, rather than the rounded look of many indicas. On the other hand, her wide, fat-bladed leaves are the classic indica dark green. The aroma of Marley's Collie combines the pungent sweet-nectar bite of Jamaican pot with a musky Afghan undertone. Her taste is very sweet, almost acrid. When toked, Marley's Collie lights a big sativa fire in the brain simultaneous with an indica fire in the belly, rather than one effect creeping up behind the other. Fittingly, this hybrid pot's stone offers peace and awareness at once.

 60/40

 simultaneous body/head high

 fruit with pungent undertone

 60 – 65 days

 ♀ Jam2 x ♂ Ort 15T7

 up to 120 g (4¼ oz.) per plant

 SOG

Matanuska Mint

Sagarmatha

 50/50

 positive & social

 minty, of course

 65 days

 Matanuska Tundra x Grey Mist

 300-325 g/m² (1 oz./ft.²) dried, indoor

Sagarmatha was in the Matanuska Tundra cycle of seed production when some friends needed to stash a number of Grey Mist plants. There was extra space in the room with the Matanuska females where the lady Grey Mist plant took refuge. The two strains made a handsome couple, so the breeders agreed to hybridize them. "Matanuska Mist" was an obvious name for their offspring, but after looking at the mature plant's turquoise leaves and tasting her deliciously minty smoke, Sagarmatha's staff changed the name to Matanuska Mint.

Matanuska Mint's leaves display an even balance of sativa length and indica thickness. Likewise, her stone displays a bit of both influences. She has been grown outdoors on America's Pacific Coast from Eugene down to Santa Cruz. Indoors, Matanuska Mint gives best results when vegetated until she shows 4-7 internodes, then grown as a multi-branch plant reaching 1-1½ meters (¾ feet) in height. Both soil and hydro are acceptable media.

Matanuska Mint's buds get crystalline and greasy. They are firm to the touch and about the size of a big cigar, giving off a sharp whiff of mint when squeezed. This is strong, fast weed that starts working after one or two tokes, and smokers may feel their eyes droop at the onset, but this is followed by a brain nova of happy energy that rides above the body stone for several hours. Perfect for a fun night out, this buzz suits playtime activities better than working hours. The menthol-like smoke goes down smooth and expands the lungs, giving it some medicinal potential for opening the airways.

Mazar

Dutch Passion

Named for the cannabis growing center in Afghanistan, Mazar-I-Shariff, this variety derives from a resinous indica descended from marijuana's motherlands, and a Skunk #1 mother that adds some of her sweet sativa traits. This plant does well outdoors in the welcoming climates of Spain or California, but her November finish at Holland's latitude encourages an indoor setup. Mazar also makes a good greenhouse plant.

Growing vigorously in either soil or hydro, Mazar tends toward a squat dwarf-conifer silhouette, a meter (3 feet) tall or less, that suits sea of green cultivation. She carries long chunky colas and thick leaves that stay green over her whole cycle. A third flowering wave comes just before harvest, so growers that are able and willing to let her continue growing may be rewarded with additional yields.

An unobtrusive pine and sandalwood aroma makes Mazar easy to conceal, and easier on the lungs and palate than other hashy varieties. This inhale full of soft incense is a quick ticket to turning up the Technicolor of psychedelic enjoyment, but may also lead to couch-lock and even heavy sleep. Smokers are slow to build up a tolerance to Mazar so this strain can be reliable as a nightcap. The occasional Mazar expresses sativa phenotypes, including a more upbeat and heady stone. Mazar won second prize in both the 1999 *High Times* and the 2002 High Life contests.

 80/20

 body stone

 earthy/soft pine

 56-63 days
early-mid Nov. outdoors

 ♀ Afghan x ♂ Skunk #1

 400 g/m² (1¹/₃ oz./ft²) SOG
indoors
300 g (10 oz.) per plant
outdoors

 SOG

Mikush

Federation Seed Co.

F ederation Seed's Mikush is a Godzilla indica. Outdoors—ideally in a spot with lots of light and a dry breeze—Mikush's huge, dark leaves convert solar energy into explosive growth, sometimes reaching 2 meters tall by 3 meters wide. Camouflage is a must. Indoors, Mikush needs big pots and plenty of room. A heavy nutrient feed that would burn other plants only increases her power. She jumps ahead of other varieties in the seedling stage and finishes by dominating the grow room, supported by bamboo poles to prevent collapse.

Indoors or out, Mikush likes it bright, dry and breezy. Low humidity (55%) reduces any chance of mold in the superdense buds, and temperatures between 15° and 30° Celsius (60° to 85° F) will produce fat and happy plants, with 23° C (73° F) as optimal. The best outdoor results have come from the windy coasts of Northern California and Southern Washington. This strain loves to root: the bigger the root the bigger the plant, so Federation recommends big pots with staking when growing indoors. A Mikush with a big root mass generally grows larger sideways, forming a bush instead of a tree. Her strong branches don't mind being cloned. When given proper conditions, this plant will astound with its yields.

Mikush is reportedly an effective Spanish Fly, producing a physical tingle from head to toe and a relaxed receptivity that puts people in the mood. It also aids with pains or tensions with its deep body stone. Mikush's smoke is smooth and caramel sweet. It has been praised by medical users for its astringent qualities that help relieve conditions such as asthma and glaucoma.

sensual, relaxed

caramel

50 days indoors
beg. Oct. outdoors

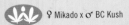

♀ Mikado x ♂ BC Kush

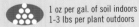

1 oz per gal. of soil indoors
1-3 lbs per plant outdoors

MK-Ultra

T.H. Seeds

Named for the notorious LSD brainwashing experiments conducted by the CIA and the Canadian police in the 1950s, MK-Ultra is secret American project pot, fathered by the rare G-13 strains. The mother is a hot indica from the City of Angels, the OG Kush. Appropriately, MK-Ultra is an unusual indica: its buzz is "bright," body-stimulating and speedy, like the body wake-up of strong tobacco or coffee.

MK-Ultra grows straight and narrow and likes to be topped. This strain stays green throughout her life. Her leaves start out fat, then get thin as they mature; her buds start off loose but get dense and hard with resin after about 40 days of flowering. MK-Ultra produces scores of small, round, popcorn-type buds. Both hydro and soil cultivation produce good yields. T.H. Seeds favors a sea of green method with 18-20 plants per square meter for this variety.

MK-Ultra has a thick, lingering aroma and a fresh pine-tree flavor that surprises with a lingering tongue-fizz, like a carbonated soda or a fizzing candy. The immediate, jolting rush is hypnotic; the extreme flavor and smell make this strain bad for sneak-a-toke, but perfect for a party icebreaker. MK-Ultra's stimulant stone can overcome body fatigue from a long night of dancing, but is a little too intense for focused work. MK-Ultra won 1st place in the 2003 *High Times* Cannabis Cup (Indica category).

 energetic, social

 fresh, piney

 53-55 days

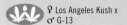 ♀ Los Angeles Kush x ♂ G-13

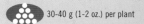 30-40 g (1-2 oz.) per plant

 SOG

Measuring Marijuana's Potency

By William Dolphin

Photo: Ed Borg

Percentages & Potency

In the world of pot propaganda, the U.S. Office of National Drug Control Policy, otherwise known as the Drug Czar's Office, claims that the potency of marijuana has risen dramatically over the last decade, making it a more dangerous drug. At one point the Drug Czar said that today's marijuana is 30 times more powerful than the weed at Woodstock. That argument was abandoned after people pointed out that the government's own measures of confiscated pot showed only a modest increase between the 1970s and the 1990s, with a 1999 average of only 4.5% THC. The average for confiscated sinsemilla is a more respectable 10% THC, but only about 4% of all the pot confiscated over the years has been "sinse"; the lion's share of confiscated pot is ditchweed.

There has always been low-THC marijuana and high-THC sinsemilla. But who likes smoking low-THC stuff? Once marijuana drops below 3% THC, the material is better suited to making rope or doormats than packing a pipe. Smoking it produces more headache than high. A 1999 study conducted by the National Organization for the Reform of Marijuana Laws (NORML) determined that the average THC content of the best medical-grade sinsemilla is 15.5%. Seed breeders who test their varieties claim results showing THC content in the high teens or even the 20% range.

What do these THC percentages really mean? And how important is THC to the quality of a high? The only way to really know what a particular plant is made of, its unique cannabinoid profile, is to employ specialized laboratory equipment – specifically, a gas chromatograph or, for ultimate precision, gas chromatography combined with mass spectroscopy.

A gas chromatograph is a complex piece of lab equipment. It can identify the chemical composition of a substance such as marijuana by separating the various chemicals it is composed of. Once the chemicals are separated, the chromatograph uses gas to send them through a thin capillary fiber known as a "column."

As the molecules exit the end of the column, an electronic detector identifies them. Generally, substances are identified by the order in which they emerge and by how long it takes to get through the column. Different molecules come through at different speeds, which is how the detector measures; it records the time at which each component reaches the outlet and the amount. Marijuana's THC percentage and its other cannabinoids can be determined through this test.

Another machine—the mass spectrometer—can be used to make a more exact measurement.

Cannabis samples for gas chromatography testing.

Photo: Ed Borg

The mass spectrometer detects the charge that results from an ion passing by or hitting a surface. When those charges are scanned, they produce a mass spectrum (hence the name). Think of the color spectrum—this test charts the rainbow of unique mass-to-charge ratios for the ions, giving a more precise picture of a strain's chemical composition.

Both of these tests are every bit as complicated and specialized as they sound. They aren't tests an amateur or hobbyist can conduct. Even highly trained and experienced technicians have difficulty measuring unfamiliar compounds. Measuring THC and other cannabinoids accurately requires a laboratory with experience in marijuana testing. In the U.S., most marijuana testing involves peeing in a cup, not finding THC concentrations. While there are labs that do this type of analysis, the risk and the cost may be prohibitive.

Practical Ways to Assess Potency

In the Garden

For those who garden their own cannabis crop, high potency plants begin with good genetics. Starting with a variety that is predisposed to high THC concentrations is key, but without adequate care, even the best genetics will fail to produce a primo plant. Marijuana gardening handbooks detail how to provide plants with the optimal nutrition, proper light, stable temperature and other factors that will help them thrive. When good quality plants are provided a healthy environment for development, potent plants will result.

Knowing when to harvest is critical to a plant's potency. There is a window when plants reach their peak ripeness. Buds plucked before fully ripening have not formed all the THC they are capable of producing. Similarly, overripe buds have degraded much of the THC to CBN, a nearly non-psychoactive cannabinoid.

Experienced growers look carefully at the heads of the trichomes that carpet the surface of a good bud, looking for the change in color from clear to amber. When somewhere between 20 and 40 percent have changed color, it's time to harvest.

How marijuana is handled after harvesting also affects potency. The trichomes, those delicate glandular heads, contain the THC. This is the "resin" or crystal coating that is prized by growers and connoisseurs. Once dried, the glands break away from the leaf very easily and are liable to be crushed accidentally. Storing pot in glass jars or other rigid containers helps to minimize the THC lost to handling. THC degrades fastest when stored in a warm, well-lit area. Keeping it in the freezer prevents degradation of potency.

In the Baggie

Most people don't grow. They rely on others for their supply, and determining the potency of dried marijuana without trying it is more art than science. A close visual inspection of dried buds and the classic "sniff" test work well, though. Buyers for medical cannabis dispensaries say feedback from patients is important. In general, what they look for is the amount of trichomes, the maturity of the pistils, the quality of the trim and cure, the smell and ultimately the taste.

Buds from a healthy, vital plant will typically be tight and bulky with a crystal content that is obvious to the naked eye; glandular formations with the THC globe on the end of the trichome stem. The best way to examine it is to use a 20x magnifying glass under fluorescent lighting. This can also reveal powdery molds that may be mistaken for crystal on casual inspection. Breaking open a bud and examining the interior is also important, as some types of mold attack from the inside.

As far as aroma, the terpenes, marijuana's aromatic chemicals, produce a range of distinctive varietal odors. Healthy plants have buds with a good, strong aroma. Some varieties are naturally more pungent than others, but not necessarily more potent. However a pleasing, pungent or floral smell is a good indication of desirable potency. Sometimes good marijuana can touch on more acrid or bitter tones, but low-quality marijuana typically has little to no aroma, or smells like hay.

Marijuana plants can sometimes surprise even the most seasoned connoisseur. A plant with great genetics that is poorly grown may not look or smell great, yet still pack a wallop. Likewise, a plant with weak genetics that has been scrupulously tended and cared for can appear far better than it is.

Of course, it's not all about THC. The potency of a particular plant reflects its chemical composition, but the enjoyment of cannabis is really so much more than sheer strength. Some people prefer pot with moderate potency, because it is easier to control just how high one gets. Once a basic level of THC potency is reached, the flavor and experience of the high are often more important than how many tokes it takes to get there.

Moroc x Afgan

Nirvana

 65/35

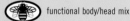 functional body/head mix

 exotic hashish

 63 days indoors
mid-Oct. in Southern Europe
outdoors

 ♀ Nirvana Afghan (P1) x
♂ strain from Ketama
region (P1)

 375-475 g/m² (1¹/₄-1¹/₂
oz./ft.²) in SOG

 SOG

This strain combines tasty strains traditionally used for hash-making—an Afghani mother and a strain from the Ketema region of Morocco. In this cross, Nirvana has created a premium variety that is reminiscent of hash in smell and flavor.

Although developed for indoor use, Moroc x Afgan (the Dutch spelling of Afghan) does well outdoors in Spain and would probably thrive in similar Mediterranean climates. The strain's Morroccan heritage favors a narrow profile for growing in cramped quarters – Nirvana recommends a sea of green with 20 plants per square meter under a 600-watt lamp. Hydro cultivation is acceptable, but soil brings out better flavor.

Moroc x Afgan shows the vigor of a strong F1 hybrid, continuing to grow long after flowering is induced. Indoors, plants put into flower at 30 cm (1 foot) achieve a final height of around 1 meter (3 feet); outdoors; 2-meter (6-foot) plants are common. This strain is roomy between its sparse limbs, which tend to bend upward more than normal. In the beginning, Moroc x Afgan's leaves look "indica," but about three weeks into flowering they become very thin and long with 7-9 leaflets. Root systems from this strain are robust. Her buds are classic "fingers," somewhat long yet very compact. The profuse trichomes are relatively even in size, giving fantastic pollinator and ice-o-lator results.

This strain is friendly to cultivate and delivers a balanced stone that is neither too sleepy nor too speedy. It serves as a perfect staple pot but the high is complex enough that it won't become boring or familiar. The exotic hybrid flavor is more apparent when cured properly and made into hash.

The NORML Conference

Usually the third week of April (4/20)

The National Organization for Reform of Marijuana Laws (NORML) has been holding national conferences since its "People's First Pot Conference" in 1972. The annual conference usually convenes in the third week of April to include the 4/20 date, if feasible. For many years, meetings were near NORML headquarters in Washington, D.C., but in recent years the flurry of cannabis activity in California enticed the meeting to San Francisco. About 300-400 activists attend the three-day event, and a handful of students are given scholarships so they can attend for free.

The NORML conference focuses on drug law reform, providing an excellent overview of the latest happenings in the U.S. marijuana legalization movement. It is a great place to network, bringing together politicians and speakers from the major reform groups, who describe their current projects and share strategic insights. Lawyers and defendants are also in attendance, and provide updates on significant cases.

At the 2004 conference, the NORML meeting was back in D.C., which allowed them to designate the first day as Congressional Lobby Day. Participants and supporters actively lobbied congress on marijuana law reform issues, then spent the remaining two days in seminars and panel discussions. The keynote speaker was Eric Schlosser, author of *Reefer Madness* and *Fast Food Nation*.

Despite the lineup of formidable activists, the NORML conference is really all about taking grassroots action. Its seminars and resources are geared to help enthusiastic citizens get involved, and to share quality information about organizing to bring about saner marijuana policy. With about 5,000 members nationally, NORML operates on a budget that is a fraction of its sibling organizations, the Marijuana Policy Project and the Drug Policy Alliance, but the strong name recognition has kept it on the front lines for the decades-long fight to reform marijuana laws.

For more information, contact NORML at www.norml.org.

New York City Diesel

Soma Seeds

Soma's New York City Diesel is a pungent sativa with incredible yields. Soma added some Hawaiian and Afghan indica influence to the popular, almost purely sativa Sour Diesel. This raises the hybrid's calyx quotient – NYC Diesel becomes a colossus of airy bud formation with very few leaves. Soma reports indoor yields of up to 100 grams per plant with some extra vegging. The strain favors indoor cultivation except in tropical climates, although good yields have been reported in the semi-arid climate of Southern California.

This strain can reach 12 feet (4 meters) outdoors or 3½ feet (150 centimeters) indoors. Soma reports best indoor results from growing NYC Diesel as a multi-branch plant in guano-fertilized soil. The plant responds well to heavy cropping, which encourages it to form four or five big top colas. NYC Diesel's few leaves are thick and wide—more palm than finger—and dark green turning more purple toward harvest. A bed or garden of these tall conifer-like ladies smells exhilarating, like a grove of ripe grapefruit. "Tart citrus" also defines their taste, a little sweeter than the mother strain's lemon tang.

Soon after the exhale, bygones will become bygones and clouds of obsessive hard feelings will be broken up by rays of sweet creative energy. NYC Diesel is a cerebral daytime toke with a hint of body stone, good for recreation and making or enjoying art. This strain has placed in three Cannabis Cups and is a popular café smoke in Amsterdam.

 60/40

 uplifting, creative, smooth

 ruby grapefruit

 70 days indoors
beg. Nov. outdoors

 ♀ Sour Diesel x
♂ Afghani-Hawaiian

 30-100 g (1-3 oz.) per plant indoors
500-3000 g (1-6 lbs.) per plant outdoors

Nirvana Special

Nirvana

The sativa-dominant Nirvana Special is for pot lovers who like a functional, creative sativa high, and plant lovers who want to organically nurture a small indoor garden yielding superior taste and potency.

Nirvana Special sprouts lanky, inquisitive branches that are easier to control when plants are grown as multi-branched rather than pruned for sea of green style gardening. Nirvana raises this strain at 12 or fewer plants per square meter under a 600-watt lamp, and starts flowering this strain when she roots, rather than holding her in vegetative growth, because she grows rapidly to fill the space. A plant put into flower at 20 centimeters will finish at over a meter. Her yield is respectable, but her flowering time is long at 11 or 12 weeks. She may produce a few male flowers during the last week of flowering.

Hydro gardening offers the best yield, up to 400g per square meter, but soil gardened crops smell and taste better. Nirvana Special leaves are medium-sized and apple green, tending toward crimson in colder environments. Rather than forming a few large colas, Nirvana Special produces fluffy popcorn buds at multiple sites. Each pocket in these buds is lined with trichomes. Organic nutrients also bring out this strain's unique sweet-sour taste, like a tart grape candy.

Nirvana Special's high dissolves apathy and laziness. It's energetic, blissful and playful. This variety can enhance an afternoon of barbeque and Frisbee, or a morning of creative work. Connoisseurs who make cannabis part of an active life will appreciate this strain's taste and buzz.

 75/25

 creative, energetic

 tart grape

 77-84 days

 ♀ Nirvana Jock Horror x ♂ sativa strain from Oaxaca, Mexico

 300-400 g/m² (1-1⅓ oz./ft²)

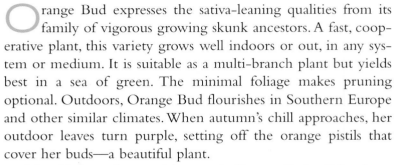

Orange Bud

Dutch Passion

80/20

up, active

orange goodness

55-65 days indoors
end Oct. outdoors

Skunks

20-25 g (³/₄-1 oz.) per plant
(SOG) indoors
200-250 g (7-9 oz.) per plant
outdoors

SOG

Orange Bud expresses the sativa-leaning qualities from its family of vigorous growing skunk ancestors. A fast, cooperative plant, this variety grows well indoors or out, in any system or medium. It is suitable as a multi-branch plant but yields best in a sea of green. The minimal foliage makes pruning optional. Outdoors, Orange Bud flourishes in Southern Europe and other similar climates. When autumn's chill approaches, her outdoor leaves turn purple, setting off the orange pistils that cover her buds—a beautiful plant.

After 30 days of vegetative growth, Orange Bud will be about 2 feet (60 centimeters) tall. Every additional week of growth will give approximately 7 inches (20 centimeters) of extra height, reaching a meter (3 feet) around harvest time indoors, or 2 meters (6 feet) outdoors. Orange Bud's leaves are classic seven-pointers. Her branches are long, and can be weighed down by the grape-like buds that grow at different sites along their length, making staking a good idea.

Orange Bud pot leaves a citrus note on the tongue, tending toward the sweet and floral like a very ripe orange or a tangerine. By the time the taste registers on the tongue, the buzz is palpable. Orange Bud is an uplifting, active mental stone, compatible with any activity. Its fast onset makes it attractive for medical relief from nausea and obsessive, distracting thoughts.

Papaya

Nirvana

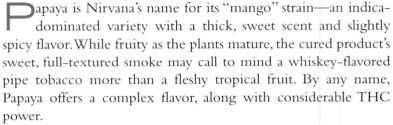

 85/15

 glazed eyes, stoney

 tropical with whiskey/tobacco tones

 56-63 days

 ♀ Citral #13 x ♂ ICE #2

 300-400 g/m² (1-1¹/₃ oz./ft²) in SOG

 SOG

Papaya is Nirvana's name for its "mango" strain—an indica-dominated variety with a thick, sweet scent and slightly spicy flavor. While fruity as the plants mature, the cured product's sweet, full-textured smoke may call to mind a whiskey-flavored pipe tobacco more than a fleshy tropical fruit. By any name, Papaya offers a complex flavor, along with considerable THC power.

Papaya is a short gal with thin, delicate branches. She will slowly double in size from flowering induction to harvest, but tends to stay low, typically under 3 meters (6 feet). Flowers are quick to form and copious, with the slightly spongy buds often forming a "nipple" at their ends. Yields range between 300 and 400 grams per square meter in a soil-based sea of green (20 plants/m²) under a 600-watt lamp. To bring out Papaya's true palate, Nirvana recommends organically-fed cultivation. Although hydroponics cultivation may yield up to 25% more, the plants will not smell or taste anywhere near as lush as their soil-based sisters.

Glazed eyes and couch-lock are almost certain to result from smoking this indica-heavy strain. Papaya is good weed for staying at home and getting absorbed into a favorite music selection or an interesting movie. It also is worth investigation for medicinal users seeking a pure and potent indica.

Passion Queen

Seedbank.com

Passion Queen is a sativa/indica hybrid notable for resin production and vigorous growth. Seedlings from this strain grow very uniformly—the sign of a stable F1 cross. Early in her growth, Passion Queen expresses sativa traits, such as narrow, widely-spaced light green leaves, but her bud production at maturity has the bulk and speed of a strong indica.

The breeders and Seedbank.com vegetate this plant for two or three weeks at most. Passion Queen can be gardened outdoors in warm climates that support a late finishing time; she can also be kept outdoors in pots. Indoors, Passion Queen will grow as a multi-branch Christmas tree sativa if given room, or she will grow as a one-cola indica if crowded in a sea of green. Either way, Her High-ness needs plenty of light and low fertilization, preferably with organics, to bring out the layers of herb and sour citrus in her palate. Passion Queen reaches 3-6 feet (1-2 meters) at maturity. She yields 400g per square meter (1⅓ oz. per square foot) from a soil or hydro sea of green, with 20-40 plants per square meter (2-4 plants per square foot).

After just a few weeks of flowering, Passion Queen displays an unusually slippery resin that is great for making hash. By maturity, the resin thickens and her flowers curl into each other and turn bluish-purple. Her buds bulk up and look finished after 8-9 weeks, but letting them ripen one more week offers a bigger, more resinous yield.

Passion Queen's fast high rises steadily for the first hour, then levels out to a stratospheric cruise for 3-4 hours of smiles and deep, pleasant thoughts. This is a good smoke for cheering up and having fun with a passionate partner. Used as vapor, this lung-cleansing herb can also relieve asthma symptoms.

 60/40

 soaring, thoughtful

 sour, herbal

 70 days

 ♀ Northern Lights x ♂ BC Grapefruit

 400 g/m² (1⅓ oz./ ft²) (SOG) indoors 4 oz.-1 lb. per plant outdoors

 SOG

Pineapple Punch

Flying Dutchmen

Photo: Cannabis College

The Flying Dutchmen's popular Real McCoy strain crosses a Hawaiian indica with Skunk #1. Real McCoy is back-crossed with its Skunk parent to produce Pineapple Punch. Interestingly, this hybrid expresses two distinct phenotypes. One is a more "sativa" pattern—tall and rangy with thin leaves and widely spaced internodes; the other is a more "indica" growth pattern, with medium-size, wider leaves, closer nodes and a slightly stronger bouquet and yield. Growers will know by the vegetative phase which trait package to expect from their plants. Both phenotypes produce the citrus taste and cerebral, active stone of their Real McCoy mother.

Outdoors, Pineapple Punch grows fairly tall with lime-colored leaves, large bracts and golden pistils. Indoors, the Dutchmen recommend growing Pineapple Punch from clones either at 12-16 plants per square meter (1-2 per square foot) unpruned or at 6-9 per square meter (1 plant per square foot), pruned once. Removing lower branches channels light and energy to the tops of the plants. Flying Dutchmen prefers soil cultivation with a 12/12 light-cycle and low to medium regimen of organic nutrients, but hydro cultivation is acceptable, too. No nutrients should be applied for at least 10 days before harvest.

Pineapple Punch's buds are medium-dense and loaded with sugary fruity resin. Her high terpene levels preserve her inviting taste and smell after water extraction, although dry sieving gives the best results. While both phenotypes offer a smooth pineapple/grapefruit smoke, the "sativas" have a sweet lavender undertone while the "indicas" are stronger and more grapefruit-astringent.

Pineapple Punch's tropical spell is likely to leave you giddy. This is a great upbeat high that brings on talkativeness and lots of grinning. A terrific accompaniment to an outdoor concert or a walk in nature, Pineapple Punch encourages a sunny perspective and offers a pick-me-up for recreational afternoons.

 70/30

 motivational, talkative, smiley

 lavender, pineapple

 63-70 days indoors
end Oct. / beg. Nov.
outdoors

 ♀ Real McCoy x
♂ Skunk#1

 300-500 g/m²
(1-1¹/₂ oz./ft.²)

 SOG

Power Plant

Dutch Passion

 80/20

 up, giddy, playful

 pungent, sandalwood, pepper

 56-63 days indoors
49-56 days or end Oct.
outdoors

 South African parents

 0.75-1 g per watt indoors
150-400 g (5-14 oz.) per
plant outdoors

 SOG

Power Plant derives from *dagga*, the sativa–dominant pot grown in South Africa and its neighboring countries. South African varieties are famous for their fast growth and early finish, in contrast to the slow growing season required by most tropical sativas. Power Plant develops almost visibly, finishing before Halloween outdoors in the Netherlands and even sooner in semi–arid, Mediterranean climates like Spain. This is a plant for growers who want strong sativa, ASAP.

Flexible and adaptive, Power Plant grows well indoors, whether in soil or hydro, multi–branched or in a sea of green. If pruned, she develops multiple compact buds that measure around 15 centimeters (6 inches) long. If she isn't pruned she grows three or four big 20–centimeter (8–inch) buds and lots of smaller popcorn. Power Plant's foliage stays olive green with thin, seven–point leaves. Her strong, pungent smell may require odor control in regions where inconspicuousness is a must. She prefers an easy hand with fertilization, and her rapid growth is very uniform: plants finish at an even 70 cm indoors (just over 2 feet), or 100 cm (3 feet) outdoors.

This power sativa's smoke tastes sharp and lights up the neural networks after a few hits. Many sativa highs can be sustained during a serious working day, but Power Plant may prove too strong for work settings. Instead, she's rocket fuel for a launch at 4:20 p.m. or later. With an uplifting, mostly mental high, Power Plant is quite compatible with dinner and freewheeling conversation; however, many sativa fans will also enjoy tripping out with a few tokes of this variety and a sketchbook or an interactive game.

Purple Skunk x Dutch Treat
East Island Seed Co.

East Island selected this hybrid for its deep flavor and gentle indica stone. "Skunk" varieties smell and taste floral but very ripe, like lavender that could compete with a skunk. Dutch Treat gives the hybrid a note of citrus fruit flavor and an unusually upbeat high for an indica-dominant plant.

Purple Skunk x Dutch Treat shows some range in physiognomy, but tends to grow short and bushy, under a meter tall on average. Her leaves are dark green, turning purple as she ripens; the same pigment occurs in many ripe large, dense buds. The robust stems of this tough little plant support heavy bud production. This variety yields best when multiple short plants are gathered in a soil-based sea of green, yielding about 2 ounces per plant in this setup. Multi-branch or hydro growing will often produce lower yields per square foot because they don't work with the plant's natural tendencies. The dank smell that wafts up from this crowd of skunky little girls may need to be masked by ozone or other security measures.

Purple Skunk x Dutch Treat bathes the mouth in heavy swirls of smoke with a sweet wildflower bite. If the smoke is savored a little before inhaling, like a fine tobacco, one may taste tones of orange or berry from the Dutch Treat father. Flavor alone is one reason people like this variety, yet the high is noteworthy, too — a very potent, fast onset muscle-loosener that stays mellow, and pleasingly trippy but not too incapacitating or zoney. This is an enhancement smoke for relaxing with friends or an easy day at the beach, and one that can be mixed with good wine or beer without forcing an early bedtime.

 80/20

 fast, mellow

 sweet, lavender, pungent

 60 days

 ♀ Purple Skunk x
♂ Dutch Treat

 55 g (2 oz.) per plant SOG

 SOG

Cannabis Harvest Cups

Mardi Grass
Usually in May, Nimbin, Australia
By Ed Rosenthal

Mardi Grass is the major mariuana festival held south of the equator. This festival's home is Nimbin, often called the Alternative Capital of Australia. Nimbin is a small community tucked into the foothills of the Tweed Volcano series in New South Wales. Since the 1970s, it has been known for its experiments in economic and social structure. Nimbin's innovations include mass use of solar, wind and other natural energy sources; a unique currency system and many sustainability projects. Also famed for its radically progressive drug policies, it has a decades-long reputation for both quality marijuana and lively marijuana celebrations and rallies.

Mardi Grass starts on the Wednesday or Thursday before the first weekend in May and lasts through the weekend. May is toward the end of Australia's harvest season, and Mardi Grass is a marijuana harvest celebration that weaves culture, fantasy, spiritualism and politics together into a raucous festival.

Although there were earlier festivals, this event got the name "Mardi Grass" in the early 1990s. At that time, about 4000 people attended the event. Now the festival draws over 20,000 people and is more organized. Planned events range from seminars to the Hemp Olympics, which started in 1996. Competitions include blindfolded, speed joint rolling, artistic joint contests,

The Plantem (cannabis cousin to The Phantom) carries out his superhero duties. Photo: Barge

A mouth-watering Mardi Grass banquet. Photo: Barge

and the notorious bong-throw. There is always musical entertainment, and awards are given for the best hemp songs and dances.

The notorious parade isn't much of a parade at all, since Nimbin is only a few blocks long and a few blocks wide. Still, loads of people in costumes wander and watch as floats pass by in a caravan, joining in the general merriment.

Nimbin is a unique community worthy of a visit, just to appreciate the social experiment this town has been enacting for over 30 years. The demographic has shifted, but the town and its annual celebration continue to insist: it is time for the larger society to adopt saner marijuana policies.

For more info: www.nimbinmardigrass.com

Samplers settle into the serious "work" of judging the best buds. Photo: Barge

The Toker's Bowl
Usually in May, Vancouver, BC
By Jaloola

Photo: Patty Mitropoulos/Cannabis Culture

Downtown Vancouver, British Columbia is the center for the Canadian west coast marijuana movement. Dubbed "Vansterdam" by those in the know, this beautiful city has a downtown neighborhood bordering the historic Gastown district where visitors can buy marijuana seeds, one-of-a-kind glass pipes and hemp clothing. Based on West Hastings Street, this small neighborhood even has a few Amsterdam-like coffeeshops, where you can smoke it if you've got it, but the sale of marijuana is still illegal. Cafes may have rules to help minimize interaction with authorities, so check before lighting up.

The Toker's Bowl is an intimate and casual affair with about 200 attendees. Sponsored by *Cannabis Culture* magazine, it features four days and nights of food, fun and festivities centered around sampling and celebrating Canada's primo homegrown. And there is plenty to compare notes about: like the 20-plus pounds of the finest Canadian weed the attendees are judging. With a judge's pass comes a sample of all the entries (23 in 2003) and some accessories to aid in the process. The next four days is a race to try each one without blurring them all together.

Winners are announced at the final party, a casual yet jubilant affair. There are also contests, music, dancing, good food and of course whatever kind smoke people are generously sharing or still finishing up. This is what the Bowl is about: good times with like minds, and rewarding the fine work of folks who have grown the best marijuana in the land.

For more info: www.tokersbowl.com

The Cannabis Cup
Typically during Thanksgiving week, Amsterdam, Netherlands

Amsterdam is the ideal vacation for the budding canna-tourist, and the *High Times* Cannabis Cup is often considered the event of the year for canna-tourism. It has become a perennial favorite for American heads who would rather be partying than spending their Thanksgiving holidays with family.

The Cannabis Cup actually struggled through its first years, with initial difficulties from within and without—but by its 8th year, the harvest event was pulling in 1,500 attendees and has only grown from there. Now heads flock to this noto-

Lovely Amsterdam. Photo: Ed Rosenthal

rious party and tastefest in the thousands from locations around the globe.

Especially at Cup time, it is good to remember that cannabis remains illegal in Holland, at least in theory. Many forget this fact; that is, if they ever knew it to begin with. There is no denying how civilized it feels to sit at a sidewalk café and light up a joint. Just be sure to show respect for this freedom and mind the basic manners that make you a welcome guest.

The daytime part of the Cup is held in an exhibition hall that is thick with smoke and filled with booths where seed companies, glass companies, and many others display their cannabis friendly products. Award competitors offer samples and freebies in an attempt to seal the popular vote. Informal seminars on marijuana topics are held all day, but are peripheral to the informal socializing, visits to the coffeeshops, and the

Hemp icon Jack Herer speaks to the Cannabis Cup crowd. In 2003, he was inducted in the Cup's Counterculture Hall of Fame. Photo: Ed Rosenthal

serious work of trying to judge all the samples (or get real stoned trying) that comprise most attendees' days.

Night events give everyone a chance to gossip, step out, hang out with Cup friends, hear the bands or dance to the tunes the DJ spins and generally keep the party mood going. The last night is always an extravaganza; after the cups are awarded, the celebration stretches into the wee hours of the night.

Every year, rumors fly about whether or how the judging is rigged; about internal politics between various companies, or even just the politics of *High Times* magazine itself. In fact, the last few years have raised serious questions about *High Times* business practices and politics. Recent changes to the magazine format have some guessing how the Cup will metamorphose as it enters its 17th year. Despite these suspicions, the Cannabis Cup remains the Disney Land of cannabis destinations. This long-standing event tops the wish list of heads worldwide.

For more info: www.cannabiscup.com

Labeled samples of Cup competitors. Judge's samples are "blind" with only numbers or letters on the label to match the sample with the ballot.

Photo: Ed Rosenthal

Rocklock

DNA Genetics

Photo: Donja

Rocklock stands on the shoulders of giants. This strain derives from a carefully selected cross of gifted genetics, RockStar and Warlock. Both parents are easy-growing indoor strains with unusually stimulating indica buzzes. Rocklock, too, offers easy cultivation and a deep and stoney but awake experience. This version of "stimulant indica" leans toward a heavy trip that doesn't have to end in the pillows.

DNA prefers Rocklock in a soil-based sea of green, fed with guano. Under these conditions she grows from 60-150 cm (2-5 feet) with a large central cola. She has more leaves (in ratio to calyxes) than some connoisseur plants, but those leaves are sweet and starry with crystals – good material for water hash. As she matures, her leaves change to a nice purple/yellow to signal that she is finished. On the whole this is a very easy strain to grow that can yield up to 30 grams per plant indoors. Rocklock has never been tested outdoors.

Rocklock smells and tastes sour-sweet, a bit like a fruity cough drop. The high feels like standing near a giant bass speaker at concert—the Rocklock vibe seethes through the whole body, warm and numbing but not sleepy. In fact, smokers of this strain are often found standing near the speakers at concerts, dissolving the self/music barrier in an indica dream. The same stone can offer relief to persons suffering from body-located tension, inflammation and pain.

 85/15

 stoney and awake

 sour candy

 55-65 days

 ♀ Rockstar x ♂ Warlock

 15-30g (¹/₂- 1 oz.) per plant indoors

 SOG

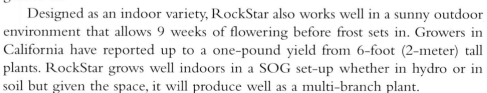

RockStar

Bonguru Beans

Photos: J. Cervantes

The "Star" in RockStar is the multi-award-winning Sensi Star, a potent indica with a slighlty cerebral, sativa-influenced stone. This Star's "Rock" is not music-related, but rather the Soma A+ mother, which is often called "Rockbud" for its super-dense buds that offer no footholds for molds and pests. "Rockbud's" compact growth genes reign in Sensi's sativa-like branching, making RockStar easier to manicure than its papa plant. This RockStar combo is a good strain for beginners and delivers buds with a rhythm that any indica fan will gladly groove to.

Designed as an indoor variety, RockStar also works well in a sunny outdoor environment that allows 9 weeks of flowering before frost sets in. Growers in California have reported up to a one-pound yield from 6-foot (2-meter) tall plants. RockStar grows well indoors in a SOG set-up whether in hydro or in soil but given the space, it will produce well as a multi-branch plant.

This strain shows her hardcore indica roots with typically fat leaves and chunky nugs. The glisten of trichomes is suitable for finger hash. Her pungent spicy fruit bouquet, a bit like a very ripe cinnamon pear, does not overpower the room during flowering. By harvest this visually striking plant is draped in crystal snow.

A full-bodied smoke in terms of taste and texture, RockStar's buzz avoids the usual indica heaviness. Users will not feel weighed down by this stone, just more limber and easygoing. RockStar's effects can help medicinal smokers who need a non-narcotic muscle relaxant. When you want to party like a RockStar, this variety loosens the mood without too much space-out factor.

 I S

 body relaxation

pungent spicy fruit

56-63 days

♀ Rock Bud x ♂ Sensi Star

450 g/m² (1½ oz./ft.²) indoors
up to 1 lb. outdoors

 SOG

117

Rox

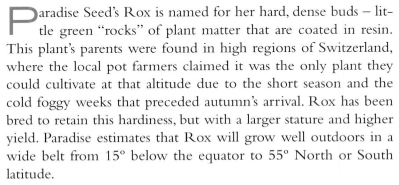

Paradise Seeds

 energetic, direct

 strawberry/mint

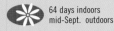 64 days indoors
mid-Sept. outdoors

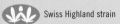 Swiss Highland strain

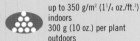 up to 350 g/m² (1¹/₄ oz./ft.²)
indoors
300 g (10 oz.) per plant
outdoors

Paradise Seed's Rox is named for her hard, dense buds – little green "rocks" of plant matter that are coated in resin. This plant's parents were found in high regions of Switzerland, where the local pot farmers claimed it was the only plant they could cultivate at that altitude due to the short season and the cold foggy weeks that preceded autumn's arrival. Rox has been bred to retain this hardiness, but with a larger stature and higher yield. Paradise estimates that Rox will grow well outdoors in a wide belt from 15° below the equator to 55° North or South latitude.

"Density" is the keyword for Rox. Her small-stature will please gardeners with limited room or security worries. By harvest she forms a conical, slightly leaning Matterhorn of buds on her main cola spiked by a few long, yucca-like leaves. Sea of green is a great system for this little tower of buds.

Rox has a sharp-sweet palate, like a strawberry so cold and sugary that it almost tastes minty. This variety gives an energetic and even jolting buzz that tends to be more strongly felt in the body's nerves than the grey matter. A good variety for the fan of potent highs, Rox often stones users with the first good hit, circulating its buzz like an electric current through the body. It often comes on so fast that it rings the ears and revs the heart in an amusement-ride type of adrenaline rush. Not a 9 to 5 smoke, Rox likes to go to parties where there will be some dancing and who knows what else as the night heats up.

118

Spannabis

Late February, Barcelona, Spain

By Ed Rosenthal

Spannabis is one of several new trade shows in Europe. The first annual three-day show took place in February 2004. As the very first major commercial cannabis event in Spain, it was considered a huge success by everyone: the producers, the exhibitors and the public.

The event was held at the Palau San Jordi. Originally built for the 1992 Olympic Games, it is the largest enclosed exhibit space in the city of Barcelona. Companies from all over Europe exhibited their wares at this event, with booths for fertilizer, lights, hydroponics equipment, paraphernalia and hemp products. Seed companies from Amsterdam, England, and Spain were also in attendance.

Spanish aficionados have a choice of two magazines, *Cañamo* and *Yerba*, an offshoot of the Dutch *High Life* Magazine. Both magazines were represented. Doctors, lawyers, authors and even a researcher from Cannabiogen gave presentations.

In Spain, possession and presumably cultivation of marijuana for personal use was recently legalized. It was inevitable that the show would happen. The citizens of Spain love their freedom and take it seriously.

Spannabis had an exuberance that other trade shows have lost. Part of it might be that the seed companies were in full attendance with more than 10 exhibitors at the show. Seed booths brighten spirits and in a sense are the heart of the show. Spannabis had plenty of kind buds and good feelings.

Find out more: www.spannabis.com

One colorful Spannabis exhibit display. Photo: Ed Rosenthal

Cannabusiness

Late September, Germany

By Ed Rosenthal

In previous years, Cannabusiness has been held in Castrop-Rauxel, a small town in the heart of the Ruhr valley of western Germany, and not far from the Dutch border.

Hendrik Düppe and Emil Reichman started the show in 1996. As it enters its 9th year Cannabiz, as it is fondly nicknamed, has a reputation to uphold. This international festival is a multi-day event that draws more than 140 exhibitors from 17 different nations, and has visitors in the thousands from dozens of countries. There are days open to non-trade visitors, but over 1,000 business visitors attend to get the latest of the latest in marijuana and hemp product innovations. There is an extensive lecture and seminar series featuring big names and experts on cannabis. Several years have also focused specifically on medical marijuana issues. DJs and other musical acts provide some entertainment that no cannabis event would be complete without.

In 2004, Cannabusiness has relocated to the Palladium, a 100-year old, former industry hall in Cologne. The fourth biggest city in Germany, Cologne is situated just south of the fair's previous home. It is considered an international center for trade fairs, and features the Cologne Dom a famous cathedral begun in 1248 that took over 600 years to build. The 2005 show, the 10-year anniversary, will be held in Berlin.

Cannabusiness features discussions, lectures and forums on health, hemp and legalization topics, but most people attend to walk around the exhibition hall and look at the extensive trade exhibits, which awes newcomers. Every conceivable bong, waterpipe and vaporizer is displayed. Growing equipment and fertilizer companies, and all kinds of growing equipment are available. Hemp products and a multitude of lifestyle products for the cannabis friendly are also plentiful.

"Old-timers" still remember the days when seed companies were at the show in numbers. Seed sales were banned by the German government in 2000. Even with the ban, the show is currently the largest of its kind in the world.

Cannabusiness marks the maturation of the marijuana industry in Europe. It has proven that there was a large enough constituency to support a large venture. The show allows the interested public to see the breadth of products available and to check out new ideas at the lectures and discussions. Its continued success shows how diverse and inventive the marijuana and hemp industry is, and that there is a market to support marijuana and hemp products.

For more info: www.cannabusiness.com

Cannabusiness, the biggest trade show of its kind. Photo: Barge

CannaTrade

Beginning of April, Bern, Switzerland

By Don E Wirtshafter

Hundreds of potted and gold-painted cannabis plants lined the walks to greet visitors to CannaTrade. The gold spray paint on the tall hemp plants was one of the few compromises the organizers of this outstanding show had to make to get the show approved by Swiss police authorities. The gendarmes must have felt they were doing their job protecting these immature, non-psychoactive fiber plants from being taken from the hall and diverted to the drug market. Good job, boys!

Just a few years ago, the Swiss scene was a source of great hope for changing marijuana policy within Europe. As we entered the new millennium, Switzerland liberalized its marijuana policy, and it looked like cannabis might be made legal. Simultaneously, Belgium legalized and Spain's policy entered a more liberal phase; England also reclassified marijuana to a lower schedule, which reduced penalties for use. In the U.S., the medical marijuana experiment seemed to be gaining ground

Photo: Barge

with more states passing initiatives, or placing the issue on their ballots for consideration. It was beginning to seem like enough global momentum was building to shift the paradigm on marijuana.

But by last year, a backlash in Switzerland led to many busts and raids. Some breeders who had expanded ventures into Switzerland barely escaped imprisonment; a few were prosecuted but let go with fines or minimum punishments; others, like Mr. Nice breeder Shantibaba, are sitting in Swiss jail.

Despite the hardships of the policy for growers in Switzerland, the Swiss CannaTrade show coasted into existence 4 years ago, and has continued to put out a premier event; at once friendly and professional.

The 2004 show moved to a new exhibition hall, where the show floor was awash with displays of growing equipment, harvesting tools, a thousand varieties of seeds and smoking accessories. Industrial hemp projects, long banned in the U.S., are progressing in Europe and

Photo: Barge

were well-represented with HempFlax of the Netherlands easily taking the honors as the most ambitious hemp company around.

Like the other main trade fairs, CannaTrade hosts a series of seminars including the latest on medical marijuana, cultivation techniques, industrial hemp and international efforts at legalization. This multilingual country provides live translations at seminars, which make it easy for English speakers to hear the variety of European experts speaking in Swiss, German, French and Italian. If you go, don't miss the event's fashion show. It's a great preview of the styles to come.

Travel and Hotel accommodations are best found on the show's excellent website: www.cannatrade.ch

Photo: Barge

T.H. Seeds

Formed as a partnership between two Americans in 1993, T.H. Seeds was originally called the C.I.A. (Cannabis in Amsterdam). Their store served as a cannabis information center and seed shop for their up-and-coming high quality strains. It was also the very first hemp store in Europe, carrying a full range of high-quality hemp clothing and products.

On the seed breeding end, T.H. Seeds has developed a solid foundation of prizewinning strains. Their determined attitude combines with their understanding of plant science to deliver consistent quality genetics. T.H. Seeds has brought "new school cannabis genetics," to Amsterdam—fresh mother and father strains taken primarily from west coast American connections—to create truly unique stable strains. They've helped expand the diversity among Amsterdam's offerings, and the special qualities of their strains have garnered them awards in many of the harvest cups throughout Europe.

T.H. Seed's home is at the Hemp Works Shop, located at Nieuwendijk 13. This is at the heart of a pedestrian shopping area within easy walking distance from Amsterdam's Central Station or Dam Square. It is common to find the breeders and gardeners from T.H. Seeds around and ready to talk shop. A real resource for the global community of serious growers, hemp supporters, and Drum 'n Bass fans, T.H. Seeds founders and staff are grower-oriented and enjoy comparing notes and getting as much feedback from people who garden their strains as possible. They also support better policies regarding pot and hemp worldwide and encourage everyone to "please discourage prohibitive, restrictive and destructive thinking on cannabis!"

Heavy Duty Fruity plants

Sage 'n Sour

T.H. Seeds

T. H. Seeds prefers a straightforward approach to marijuana genetics, so they named this strain directly for its parentage. SAGE (Sativa-Afghan Genetic Equilibrium) is the male used in this hybrid. SAGE's balance of potency, hardiness and flavor have won this strain several awards. It has also been registered as a medicinal cannabis by the British government. Its distinctive Haze-dominant traits in flavor, smell and strength make it perfect to breed with the Sour Diesel, a very popular female clone from New York. Sour Diesel has a lemony sour flavor and a near-cult following at home.

Sage 'n Sour likes heavy nutrient feeding in soil or hydro. This brings out her explosive multi-branch growth. As she surges toward her 1½ meter (4½ feet) indoor height, she stacks up dark green flowers and resinous spade-shaped buds. She tends to grow a little bent, adjusting to the weight of her abundant colas. During growth, this variety smells clean and sagey like her father, making odor control less of a worry. With heavy feeding and good light, yields of 500 grams per square meter are not uncommon.

The Sage 'n Sour high is a fast, euphoric wake-up good for socializing. She doesn't tire you out like so many indica-influenced strains. The smoke tastes and smells like sandalwood incense dusted with lemon. With a lip smacking aftertaste and a hard-hitting yet smooth high, you and your friends will remember this variety like a little taste of summertime.

  75/25

 awake, euphoric

 sage, sandalwood, lemon

 63-70 days

 ♀ Sour Diesel x ♂ SAGE

 300-600 g/m² (1-2 oz./ft.²)

Sapphire Star

Jordan of the Islands

Sapphire Star is a berry-flavored, haze-influenced cross from a popular Hawaiian sativa strain and the powerful indica God Bud. Like a pure sativa, Sapphire Star bushes out in all directions, reaching a looming 5-6 feet indoors and up to 15 feet outdoors. Her stone also displays classic sativa traits—a blissful flight of ideas takes off fast from a few tokes. But the God Bud indica influence shortens Sapphire Star's flowering time considerably from the sativa norm, as well as sweetening the musky taste.

Indoors, Sapphire Star needs regular feeding to get the best growth from either soil or hydro crops. Sea of green planting may be possible for an experienced gardener who can prune and cull the bushy plants. Sapphire's foliage often looks speckled with dew as she flowers—this is actually quite watery resin, which makes it easy to collect as finger hash. Sapphire Star's buds are small but dense and well-shaped. Outdoors, her fast finish and awesome size in Canada offer good prospects for outdoor growth in other cold climates.

Imagine a patch of blueberries dripping sap over blooming thistles and musky Bermuda grass—that berry-and-weed combination is Sapphire Star's bouquet from the grow room to the pipe to the exhale. Her uplifting high makes for happy, fluent conversation. Light housework or heavy petting are also recommended with this energetic smoke.

 60/40

 alert, cerebral

 skunky berry

 49-56 days indoors
end Sept. outdoors

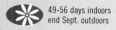 ♀ Blue Hawaiian sativa x
♂ God Bud

 4-6 oz. per plant indoors
5-10 oz. per plant outdoors

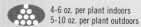

 SOG

126

Sativa Spirit

Paradise Seeds

 uplifting, energetic

 fruity

 65-70 days indoors
late Oct. outdoors at
45° latitude N

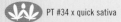 PT #34 x quick sativa

 500g/m² (1½ oz./ft.²)
indoors
700g (24 oz.) or more per
plant outdoors

The spirit of sativa is a spirit of joy and abundance. In this variety, Paradise has harnessed the bounty of sativa euphoria into an unusually hardy and tractable classic plant that is easy to grow indoors or out. Her monster yields are "sativa" in every respect, and will have fans of uplifting smokes putting her on their keeper list.

For a plant with equatorial origins, Sativa Spirit fares very well in cold climates, reportedly as far North as 50° latitude—although between between 45° North and 15° South is a safer bet for finishing early enough to avoid frost. These plants grow tall and lanky, sporting long prehensile buds that look like they've been dipped in sugar because of their profusion of trichomes. An outdoor yield of over 700 grams per plant is not unusual. Indoors, Paradise prefers to garden this tall sativa in a sea of green, for an average yield of 500 grams per square meter. Soil or hydro is an acceptable indoor medium.

Sativa Spirit is a pleasure smoke. With a taste like dark berries or red grapes, this strain has a smooth inhale and the energetic buzz comes on fast. Smokers will crave active recreation, like a trip to the beach or a nightclub, rather than staying locked to the couch and glued to the tube. This high also motivates adults to finish their chores—routine non-hazardous tasks like cleaning, filing, and gardening. It's a happy high that can lighten the mood and spark creativity.

Satori

Mandala Seeds

Satori is a gentle sativa that opens the doors of perception. She's also a huge yielder, indoors or out, in soil or in hydro. Satori seedlings grow thin—tall angels with tough main stems. However, height is not a stabilized trait in this hybrid—for example, her outdoor growth varies from 2 to 3 meters (6-9 feet). Growers with headroom or camouflage concerns can prune Satori's main stem during early growth, and the pruned plant will cheerfully expand as a short, multi-branch sativa with no loss of yield. The lateral branches reach 30 cm (1 foot) outdoors, never sub-branching unless trimmed for cuttings. During early flowering, her branches stay upright and close to the central cola. Later some support may be necessary because rock-heavy buds develop along the branch tips and bend them down.

All the buds that sprout from Satori's tips are first-rate, whether grown on the long central cola that takes up 40% of her main stem, or on her very bottom branches. Dense, pagoda-like buds accumulate on branch tips, with still more small buds tucked behind them. Resin production is low until the closing stages of flowering, about 3 weeks before harvest. At this point a coat of bright, glistening resin appears on the conical buds. Under a magnifying glass one can already see why Satori is so transcendent—her exceptionally long stalked trichomes remain translucent right up till harvest, preserving high levels of THC. Wise growers will be patient with her long flowering period as her constant production of buds makes bumper harvests routine.

In Japanese, "satori" means a moment of enlightenment in daily life. Satori's aromatic honey-herbal smoke has a fresh tinge that evokes thyme, oregano and pine. This variety aids access to those bliss moments when seeing, knowing, and loving the world are the same. The breeder recommends Satori for consciousness-expanding experiences and artwork.

 blissful, spiritual

 honey-herbal

 70-75 days indoors
Nov. outdoors

 ♀ Lucid Dreams x
♂ unnamed sativa hybrid

 500-600g/m² (1¹/₂ - 2oz./ft.²)
indoors
up to 500g (17oz.) per plant
outdoors

 SOG

Shiesel

Bonguru Beans

 75/25

 narcotic, trippy

 exotic fruit

 63-70+ days, variable

 Shiva x New York Diesel

 moderate

 SOG

Shiesel was bred for a combination of taste and stone. The effects come mostly from the Shiva parent – body-located but profound and hashy. First-time users will be patting the walls for support and may find themselves standing agape, staring at the contents of the refrigerator. The Shiesel flavor is a sweet-and-sour handful of dried fruit from the strain's papa, NYC Diesel. The potency of the Shiva combined with the exotic palate of the Diesel offers a plethora of delights for the connoisseur.

This variety thrives whether grown in a hydroponics or soil setup. She may look diminutive at first, but this short girl will experience a late growth spurt, climbing a meter in height partway through flowering. Certainly her colas exhibit the massive size and crystally blanket of glands that are characteristic of her Shiva pedigree. Shiesel needs steady feeding and patience during her 9-to-10-week-plus flowering time but growers will want those extra weeks of resin production that is apparent by the growing dank sweet odor verging on acrid.

Shiesel enhances being in the flesh, with its nearly narcotic body stone. Many smokers will be there with one good hit. Not an enhancement pot for social effervescence, this bud is better served up with low lighting, down tempo grooves and furniture that encourages lounging. Passing around a bong or joint of Shiesel brings a hushed reflection over the room, as each person spaces out on their own mental exploration or sinks into a quiet awareness of their senses.

Photo: Marco

Shiva

Homegrown Fantaseeds

Traditionalist Hindus never carve statues of the god Shiva, instead representing him only by a smooth stone lingam or phallus. This symbolizes the (pro)creative powers of the lord of the dance and his many consorts. In the marijuana family epic, Shiva is a power indica from Afghanistan cultivated in the 1980s at Holland's famed Cannabis Castle. In the past twenty years, countless pot hybrids have been bred from Shiva, including the popular Shiva Skunk and Shiva Afghani strains. Homegrown Fantaseeds offers a pure Shiva strain selected for growing ease and outdoor hardiness. They recommend Shiva for every grower who wants a strong indica, but this strain's illustrious breeding history should especially attract pot botanists.

While Shiva flourishes indoors in hydro setups, the breeder prefers a soil-based sea of green. Even new growers will find this strain easy to manage. The main pitfall with Shiva is overfertilization – keep the EC level below 1.20. Shivas can be put outside for the summer without shocking them, in all but very cold climates. Shiva sports dark mint leaves and small, nuggetlike buds. Indoor yields of 25 grams per plant are common after a 9 week flowering cycle.

Homegrown Fantaseeds suggests that the Shiva smoker will be too stoned to care about the pot's taste and aroma. Nevertheless, as one's ego floats into the dark spaces between the stars, running one's tongue over teeth may yield shafts of pointy-sharp pure weed taste and electrical cardamom spiciness. Shiva offers tokers a strong body-driven stone for use as a relaxation tool at the end of the day.

 body stone

 pungent, spicy

 60-65 days

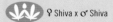 ♀ Shiva x ♂ Shiva

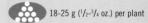 18-25 g (¹/₂-³/₄ oz.) per plant

Skydog

Willy Jack

Skydog is an F1 hybrid from Willy Jack's seedbank. Willy Jack likes F1 plants because they are more vigorous growers. Skydog mixes some haze ancestors with strong indicas selected for fast growth, THC content and a balance between mental and physical stones. Above all, this cross is potent. Smokers will fly out the chimney with both mind and body vibrating to Skydog's song.

Skydog exhibits balanced, rapid growth in a sea of green. She reaches 3½ feet indoors with a compact profile and sturdy branching. Skydog flowers quickly, filling her growing area with an intense lemon scent. While this strain generally finishes in around 8 weeks, some plants may express more Haze genes, which means stretchy branch growth and a slower finish. Growers may find it worthwhile to ripen a stretchy plant for an extra two weeks, giving her time to brew an even more floaty, mental, sativa-flavored high. These plants are real calyx factories, producing big bud clusters crystalline with resin.

Outdoors, Skydog finishes early enough to avoid Jack Frost, even in Canada. But she is sensitive to bad weather, so she should be watched as the weather turns chillier. This variety's normally green leaves tend toward a red pigment outdoors. However the leaves are not very noticeable on a mature Skydog, as they will be overwhelmed by a coral-like proliferation of buds.

Some tokers rate Skydog among the strongest of all Canadian strains. This is a mental vacation smoke, but one that's giddy rather than lethargic. It's a good choice for a godlike morning walk in alpine meadows followed by a long come-down toward lunch. It would also go well with a one-man-army computer game and something loud on the headphones.

 70/30

 even head/body stone

 lemon

 55-60 days indoors
end Sept./ beg. Oct. outdoors

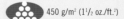 Skydog

 450 g/m² (1½ oz./ft.²)

SOG

133

Quality and Yield

By Ed Rosenthal

Yield is the obsession of many gardeners. How much will a plant produce? That may seem like a simple question, but there are many facets. For indoor gardeners, space, watts and time are considerations. For outdoor gardeners space, shape and ripening time are of concern. Raw numbers don't tell the whole story. Quality is also a factor. Less herb with better qualities is often preferable to more mediocre stash.

Indoor gardeners often refer to yield per watt. A half-gram to gram per watt of light is a good average expectation, but maturation time must also be taken into account. If a variety requires 90 days to mature, delivering a gram per watt, it has required 50 percent more flowering time than the variety that ripen in 60 days.

Why choose a late ripening variety? Most gardeners choose what to cultivate for its essence: it approximates an ideal of the effects they desire or think are desireable; basically, it is herb that leads in directions they want to go.

Yield is determined by both genetic and environmental factors. The genes set the potential, the blueprint for its life plan. The environment determines how well the plant's needs are met and thus how close it will come to its genetic potential.

The plant's growth pattern, flowering and ripening time, bud size, quality, odor, taste and high are all genetically programmed. Similar to grapes made into wines, all samples of a particular variety will have a somewhat similar flavor. However, plants of the same genetic stock produce their own unique flavors when grown in different places or under different conditions. The interplay between genetics and environment results in the unique properties of each harvest.

The best way to assure high yield of superior produce is to plant the best varieties adapted to the environment you are using. An adapted variety will perform closer to its potential. Plants that have to adapt to unsuitable environments may struggle and perform below expectations.

So what are the environmental factors that influence plant growth? The main ones are light, nutrients, temperature, water and CO_2. Each of these plays a role in plant growth: control them and you are on the road to producing the finest flowers.

Photo courtesy Paradise Seeds

Luc of Paradise Seeds wheeling in the buds.

Light-Plants use light to fuel photosynthesis. This process creates sugar, which is used for energy and tissue building. You could say that light equals growth. The more light the plant receives, the more sugar is available for tissue growth. Plants growing under otherwise identical conditions will produce more tissue growth when more intense light per square foot is provided, so long as temperature remains in the acceptable range. A plant in full sun produces more—and better quality—than one in part shade.

UV light plays a role in THC production. As the UV-B spectrum intensifies, THC content of quality strains will also rise. Plants cultivated at higher altitudes or harvested during mid-summer have higher THC content than low altitude or fall-ripened plants.

Nutrients-To function and grow, plants need nutrients. Their needs change as the plant moves through its life cycle. Nitrogen, phosphorus and potassium are the building blocks, and can be seen on fertilizer labels in the abbreviation N-P-K. When plants are denied a balanced supply of nutrients, their growth is impeded. Plants tell you what they need, you just have to understand their language. Every deficiency and toxicity condition has readily identifiable symptoms. Just read a good grow book, or a few, to learn the language of the leaves.

Temperature-Indoors and out, plants do best at moderate temperature, in the mid-70s F (low 20s C). When the temps drop below that, growth suffers because metabolism slows down. At higher temps, the buds and flowers become misshapen and stretch. Of course, varieties differ in their preferences and tolerances to heat and coolness.

Water-Indoors, water quantity is usually not a concern, but sometimes water quality can be a problem. Outdoors, nature can be too stingy or too generous with her watering program. This impacts yield. However, some of the impact can be mitigated by preparing your garden for the unexpected drought and finding out about water quality.

Carbon Dioxide (CO_2)-During photosynthesis, plants combine CO_2 from air with water to form sugar. The amount of CO_2 in the air influences the rate of photosynthesis. The atmosphere typically contains a concentration of CO_2 at about 375 parts per million (ppm). As the level drifts down to 200 ppm, photosynthesis gradually grinds to a halt. When air is enriched with CO_2 (and there is sufficient light), the photosynthesis rate rises, more sugar is produced, and plants grow bigger, faster and produce more flowers. Enriching indoor gardens with CO_2 is the cheapest environmental method of increasing yield and shortening ripening time.

Slyder

Sagarmatha

 I

 very sedating

 discreet

 55-60 days

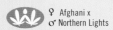 ♀ Afghani x
♂ Northern Lights

 300-325 g/m² (1 oz./ft.²)

 SOG

In the 1980s, just after the Soviet Union withdrew from Afghanistan, a cannabis explorer from Amsterdam set off to meet the traditional ganja farmers of the Khyber Pass. She gained their trust by sharing stashes with them, and returned home with a selection of rare Afghan seeds chosen for their sedative qualities. Traditional hash strains like these tend to be acclimated to Afghanistan, thus ill-suited for either indoor growth or for outdoor conditions in the Netherlands. But crossing the Afghan seeds with Northern Lights resulted in an ideal indoor-adapted sedative indica, Sagarmatha's Slyder.

Dutch growers vegetate Slyder until she produces between four and seven internodes, at which point they clip her central cola. She does equally well as a multi-branch or sea of green plant, yielding over 300 grams per square meter in SOG cultivation. At maturity, Slyder is a compact one-meter plant with conifer-like features, dark olive foliage, and pine-cone-like buds that shimmer with golden highlights and the amber hues of resin. Despite Slyder's robust production, her perfume is too faint to cause odor security worries.

As Sagarmatha says, Slyder can be "kept in the medicine box for when smokers feel anxiety, sleeplessness, post-traumatic stress or a desire for zombie-like behavior." It's not a working-hours smoke. The smoker's arms and legs acquire a warm heaviness that feels just right on a sofa but makes walking seem like a nuisance, unless it's to the fridge and back. The short-term memory appointment book is blank. One becomes passive and suggestible but too sleepy to get in much trouble.

Snow White

Nirvana

 65/35

 relaxing

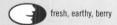 fresh, earthy, berry

 60-70 days

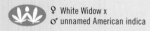 ♀ White Widow x
♂ unnamed American indica

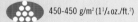 450-450 g/m² (1¹/₄ oz./ft.²)

Nirvana bills its Snow White strain as "a beautiful plant to watch grow." Depending on the light, she reaches 30-36 inches of height in a pleasing, compact bonsai spruce shape. Resin appears on the leaves just two weeks into flowering. Her dark jade pigment shows off the daily accumulation of frost as she is slowly overwhelmed by massive, sugar-coated bud production. Snow White is a variety for those seeking easy indoor cultivation, great yields, and a stone that sedates without being draining.

Snow White performs best in a sea of green hydro system. Soil cultivation is possible but will mean a less spectacular yield. Snow White shows sex slowly but flowers with stability and has very few incidences of hermaphroditism. Though not skunky, the odor can be powerful and medicinal. She shows only moderate resin early on, but truly earns her name during the last two weeks of flowering with an almost overnight coating of snow. Some growers extend her cycle an extra week for more resin production. Yields of 450 grams per square meter in a sea of green under a 600-watt lamp are very common.

Snow White's palate suggests fresh, upturned soil mixed with a medicinal smell that leans toward turpentine in astringency. Like her White Widow mother, Snow White offers a gentle and mind/body balanced high, compatible with a restaurant meal and a movie. Her father, a nameless indica from Las Vegas growers, nudges the high toward sedation. But the kiss of Snow White doesn't drop smokers to the floor and it doesn't get boring, either. Snow White will please medicinal users and other routine smokers who need relaxation without narcosis.

Soma's Amnesia Haze

Soma Seeds

Soma's Amnesia Haze is bred from Afghani, Hawaiian and Thai varieties, intermingling the special qualities of island cannabis with the enduring traits retained from its mountainous home turf. The sativa-haze dominance in the parentage requires an extended cultivation time that the Afghani only slightly mitigates. However, the smile-inducing high may be why this strain has gained such an avid fan base around Amsterdam.

Outdoors, Amnesia Haze likes the tropics; indoors, she needs an experienced hand, and prefers a roomy space, or better yet, a greenhouse. She does equally well in soil and hydro, although Soma prefers soil fertilized with guano and other organic products.

Haze is tall, expansive, and likes to branch out, forming more calyx than leaf. Her few leaves start off thick and green but look like purple crinkled paper by harvest. The blooms start small and slowly accumulate many promising white hairs during her 13-week indoor flowering cycle. By the finish, this strain's trichome hairs are unusually lengthy. Each plant rewards the diligent gardener with yields of up to 50 grams (1¾ ounces) of high end bud.

The Thai/Haze heritage lends a clean, slightly orange taste and a high that reminds users of the first time they got ripped smoking Thai stick. The texture of this experience builds slowly to a euphoric forgetfulness suitable for partying. The name of this variety comes from its ability to induce an intense buzz that often fragments short-term memory momentarily, and users should bear this in mind before undertaking any tasks that rely on a fluid connectedness of one's thoughts. Amnesia Haze may relieve chronic pain and inflammatory conditions like multiple sclerosis. In 2004, she won 1st place in the First Annual *International Cannagraphic* Growers' Cup in Amsterdam.

 70/30

 creeper, euphoric

 Thai stick

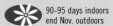 90-95 days indoors
end Nov. outdoors

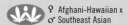 ♀ Afghani-Hawaiian x
♂ Southeast Asian

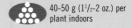 40-50 g (1½-2 oz.) per
plant indoors

139

Sour Diesel

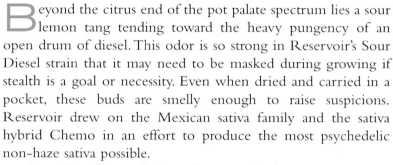

Reservoir Seeds

90/10

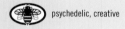
psychedelic, creative

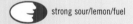
strong sour/lemon/fuel

75-80 days

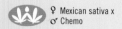
♀ Mexican sativa x
♂ Chemo

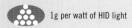
1g per watt of HID light

SOG

140

Beyond the citrus end of the pot palate spectrum lies a sour lemon tang tending toward the heavy pungency of an open drum of diesel. This odor is so strong in Reservoir's Sour Diesel strain that it may need to be masked during growing if stealth is a goal or necessity. Even when dried and carried in a pocket, these buds are smelly enough to raise suspicions. Reservoir drew on the Mexican sativa family and the sativa hybrid Chemo in an effort to produce the most psychedelic non-haze sativa possible.

Sour Diesel is a tall, thin plant suitable for sea or screen of green. She stretches in the first 3 weeks of flowering. By maturity she reaches a daunting 6 feet indoors in a slender version of the classic Christmas tree silhouette. Her foliage purples as it ages, and commonly displays pink-hued pistils. The buds are loose and spear-shaped.

Reservoir prefers Sour Diesel indoors in soil with 5.8-6.0 pH. Bloom boosters, along with a normal fertilizer regimen, can help economize her flowering time. This variety's Mexican heritage responds well to a toasty, slightly arid environment, up to 88° F with added CO_2. Warmth and plenty of light will encourage her calyxes and their penetrating, robust bouquet.

Sour Diesel's taste combined with its effects may be considered an "extreme sport" version of cannabis. The stone pulls smokers into the sky fast with a viscerally uplifting pleasure and lots of consciousness expansion in the direction of spirituality. The high lasts for the better part of an afternoon, so it is great for a creative day at home, a music show, or meditations in the woods, but incompatible with heavy machinery. This good-vibe variety may help alleviate chronic depression, as well as the ordinary blahs by encouraging a change in perspective.

StarGazer

Delta-9 Labs

StarGazer is an indoor strain from a family of strong, stoney connoisseur pot. Her mother hybridizes the indica-dominant Warlock and the sativa-dominant AK-47, both noted for fast, stimulating, and slightly hashy highs. Her Sensi Star father is likewise popular for its fast indica body stone with a side dish of mental stimulation. Between them, StarGazer's three immediate ancestors boast an average THC content of 20% and have won eleven major awards, including the High Life and *High Times* Cannabis Cups. As her name suggests, StarGazer was bred for intense, alert effects that are felt in both the mind and body; for happily gazing at the stars on a night ramble or gazing into a dance partner's eyes.

In its recommended indoor setting, StarGazer takes between 8 and 10 weeks to flower depending on the temperature. She likes cold temperatures more than most plants do, which might make her a good candidate for outdoor planting in the northern latitudes. Typically, though, StarGazer grows well in densely planted soil or hydro. Her skunk and Afghan dominated genes lead to extensive branching, but sea of green cultivation is possible with some pruning. StarGazer's internodes are close together, sprouting thin, whip-like branches that may require support once the buds begin to reach their full density. Her short, thick leaves are speckled with the oh-so-feminine pink hairs characteristic of her Warlock and AK-47 mother-line.

While she blooms, StarGazer's scent is strong and leans toward pungency. Once cured, the palate is hard to describe—in the background, creamy and slightly sour body; in the foreground, a bite of Sensi Star's lemon flavor pushed toward the astringent and minty. Delta-9 suggests that this sour-sweet mixture tastes a bit like a peppermint breath candy, such as Mentos™.

I S 80/20

relaxed, good mood

peppermint Mentos™

60-70 days

♀ Warlock (40%) x
♀ AK-47 (20%) x
♂ Sensi Star (40%)

300-500 g/m²
(1-1²/₃ oz./ft.²)

SOG

141

Strawberry Cough

Dutch Passion

 80/20

 happy medium

 strawberry

 56-63 days

 unknown

 15-25 g (¹/₂-1 oz.) per plant

Strawberry Cough is a sweet-flavored indoor variety with just enough indica influence to shorten the typically slow growing time of the semitropical sativa into a two-month flowering cycle. The creamy berry taste combines with its expansive smoke to deliver a variety worthy of its name.

Strawberry Cough gardens efficiently whether using hydroponics or soil setups. It is too branchy for sea of green, but Dutch Passion recommends planting 15-20 plants per square meter (1-2 plants per square foot). Strawberry Cough likes a boost of nutrients at the beginning of vegetative growth. Although no data was available for outdoor gardens, Strawberry Cough performs terrifically in greenhouses.

Strawberry Cough is a plant of happy mediums, growing to a height of around 3 feet indoors or in a greenhouse garden and exhibiting leaves that balance between indica and sativa influences. This multi-branched plant will start delivering ripe colas about 40 days into flowering, and continue with a second wave that finishes at about 65 days. Greenhouse flowering times are typically a week shorter than indoor gardens.

The buds are tight and shaped like narrow pinecones, and may get quite long. This variety's branches are sturdy and support even the weightiest of colas. Strawberry Cough tickles the lungs with her creamy-sweet smoke, whose flavor resembles strawberry, perhaps with a kiwi fruit complement. The buzz is heady and active, a classic let's-go-hiking sativa lift that can alleviate depression.

Additional Cannabis Events

Everywhere around the globe, cannabis brings people together. Sometimes it's in the name of science or medicine, sometimes politics, and sometimes it is simply for fun. One thing is for certain: this loose community of the cannabis friendly is as diverse and ubiquitous as the plant itself.

Festivals

Most of these events feature speakers, music, and booths with hemp-friendly wares.

Jacksonville Hempfest (Jaxhempfest)
Details: Free one-day event
Where: Jacksonville, Florida
When: Usually in spring
To find out more:
www.jaxhempfest.com

Ohio Hempfest
Details: Daylong event
Where: Columbus, Ohio
When: June
To find out more:
www.ohiohempfest.org

Planetary Pride Hempfest
Details: Long weekend, tickets needed
Where: Northern Ontario, Canada
When: late August
To find out more:
www.planetarypride.com
www.hempfest.ca
tel: 1-888-215-8970

FreedomFest
Details: Three-day event
Where: North of Barrie, Ontario, Canada
When: early August
To find out more:
www.freedom-fest.com
tel: 1-866-774-7755

HanfParade
Details: Daylong, free
Where: Berlin, Germany
When: August
To find out more:
www.hanfparade.de
tel: +49 (0)30 247-202-33

Festival du Chanvre
Where: Paris, France
When: November
To find out more:
www.festival-du-chanvre.com

Legalize! Street Rave
Where: Amsterdam and other cities
When: first weekend of June
To find out more:
www.legalize.net
info@legalize.net

Trade Shows

The focus of trade shows is generating business relationships, but these events are open to the general public and fun to attend, with only a minimal entrance fee.

Interhanf Berlin Hemp Fair
Where: Berlin, Germany
When: September
For more info:
www.interhanf.com
info@interhanf.com

London Hemp Fair
Where: London, England
When: October
For more info:
www.londonhempfair.com
info@londonhempfair.com

International HighLife Hemp Fair
Where: Utrecht, Holland
When: Spring (month varies)
For more info:
www.highlife.nl

HighLife Fair, Barcelona
Where: Barcelona, Spain
When: Fall
www.highlife.nl
bart@highlife.nl

Sugar Babe

Paradise Seeds

 fun, uplifting

 lemon, metal

 54-60 days indoors
beg. Oct. outdoors

 Afghan indica x Swiss white strain

 400-450 g/m² (1½ oz./ft²) indoors
400 g (15 oz.) per plant outdoors

Sugar Babe is the result of a union between a traditional indica hailing from the region of marijuana's purported birthplace and a mixture of Swiss-developed strains that migrated to the Netherlands after Swiss cannabis decriminalization efforts failed in the 1990s. The Afghan/Swiss combination in this darling of the Paradise collection offers growers a fast-finishing, heavy yield of potent, non-drowsy indica.

Like many Afghan-influenced strains, Sugar Babe adapts well to most outdoor areas, finishing by October in Northern Europe. The best outdoor yields, however, are found closer to the equator, between 40° North and 15° South latitudes. Sugar Babe would probably also flourish outdoors in Mediterranean climates like California and Australia. When cultivated inside, Sugar Babe ripens over a flowering cycle of 9-10 weeks, delivering about 400 grams per square meter (1½ ounces per square foot).

By the time she is harvested, Sugar Babe's buds are dense and powdery white with trichome frost. She truly looks as "sugar frosted" as the Alpine mountaintops where she originated. Her smoke takes herbal sweetness into the astringent zone—lemony, metallic and cleansing to the palate. Although indica dominates her genes, this variety's stone is a departure from the standard, delivering a powerful body high that rarely induces napping. Instead, the buzz encourages activities, and is especially great for any recreations in the great outdoors.

Super Shit

Seedbank.com

Several years ago, a friend from the U.S. gave Seedbank.com this variety, insisting that it was a "must-try" strain derived from the original skunk line. Skunk remains a popular parent strain because of its light and sweetly floral flavor that directly contradicts its name. The gardeners at Seedbank.com grew out the seeds from their friend, and agreed: the resulting plants had a wonderful sweet aroma with a mellow and stimulating high to match.

Outdoors, Super Shit fares well in moderate climates. It grows extremely fast in the vegetative stage so these plants should not be started until early summer to avoid overgrowth. The heavy branches and stiff stems quickly thicken to support the bud formations. These plants can easily reach 10 feet under the regular sun.

Super Shit grows best indoors in a sea of green or in bigger pots. When seeds are flowered early, this strain will form one primary cola; otherwise, expect branching. This plant will gobble up fertilizer and grow like mad! After 8 weeks Super Shit is essentially finished, but allowing it to grow for 10 weeks induces much heavier flowering. Seedbank.com recommends two days of complete darkness at the end of the cycle for maximum resin production. Indoors, the yield will be about 400 grams per square meter.

Super Shit grows fairly dense, fat round buds that exude a citrus pine scent. Plenty of resin is found on leaves and stems—something for hash fans to get their hands on. The high qualifies as a one-hit wonder. Long lasting and deep, it usually induces heavy sleep afterwards, making it a good strain to save for those nights when the plan is to seriously K.O., or when insomnia strikes. It also stimulates the appetite.

lethargic, munchies

citrus pine

60-70 days

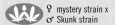
♀ mystery strain x
♂ Skunk strain

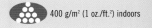
400 g/m² (1 oz./ft.²) indoors

Swiss Bliss

Paradise Seeds

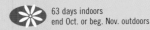
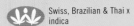

S I 75/25

blissful

tutti frutti

63 days indoors
end Oct. or beg. Nov. outdoors

Swiss, Brazilian & Thai x
indica

400 g/m² (1 oz./ft.²) indoors
up to 1000 g (2 lbs.) per
plant outdoors

Swiss Bliss is a lucky plant. Her female parentage came to Holland via a Swiss Family Robinson adventure of loss, captivity, exile and a happy ending.

This plant continues to demonstrate perseverance, growing tenaciously in many garden settings. As with many sativa strains, Swiss Bliss forms abundant limbs. Paradise likes to maintain a multi-branch plant, but prune so that the plant's energies are focused on a few budding sites, which should make for more concentrated flowers, and easier manicuring. When this lady is given the room she needs to spread her limbs, she can yield up to 400 grams per square meter (The long, sticky buds that appear will reach ripeness in about 9 weeks inside, or around November 1 when grown in Holland. Although Swiss Bliss is a survivor in the great outdoors, with commendable hardiness for a delicate sativa, the long flowering period encourages most gardener who reside more than 35° North or South of the equator to keep this gal as an indoor plant.

Swiss Bliss has a charmingly sweet aroma and a very tropical, fruit cocktail flavor. The high is ecstatic, joyful and active. The strain is a tasty companion for concerts or lively events. She also makes a great smoke for weekend adventures.

The Swiss Bliss Saga

Swiss Bliss descends from a single Swiss sativa brought to Paradise Seeds in Switzerland in the early 1990s. At the time, many established breeders had begun work in Switzerland anticipating a liberalization of that country's cannabis laws. But the Swiss government reversed course and raided Paradise's Swiss facility. The gendarmes kept Swiss Bliss's mother in a greenhouse, where she stayed in captivity for months pending a decision as to whether the plants were legal. Fortunately, the Swiss police took good care of the plants, and they coped well during their time under official protection. Indeed, it may come as no surprise to cop-savvy readers that a particularly cannabis-friendly Swiss police officer took more than a custodial interest in the powerful sativa. This secret pot activist 'topped' the plant, returning it in the form of an unrooted clone to Holland where this refugee received asylum, returning to Paradise's breeding stock.

Tanzanian Magic

African Seeds

 S

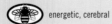 energetic, cerebral

 coal tar, licorice

 42-56 days

 Southern Highland Tanzania sativa

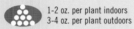 1-2 oz. per plant indoors
3-4 oz. per plant outdoors

African Seed's latest strain is the genuine article—a 100% pure sativa native to the southern highlands of Tanzania, the same region where tea is grown for the Indian ocean trade.

Tanzanian Magic has a unique, fixed flowering period that is faster than other sativas. It autoflowers, so it can't be forced by the hours of light in the day, but automatically enters the flowering cycle after it has grown for a set amount of time. Typically flowering starts after about 6-8 weeks of vegetative growth. The average African sativa grown outdoors in its region of origin stays in the vegetative growth cycle for as long as 20 weeks before entering flowering.

The leaflets are pencil thin and the overall plant stays short and bushy with compact buds. Tanzanian Magic stands about 3 feet tall when it enters flowering, and will not increase much in size during this period. The flowering cycle lasts another 6-8 weeks outdoors for a start-to-finish grow time of 12-16 weeks. This variety does better than most sativas in cooler outdoor climates. Yields from outdoor plants range from 3-4 ounces to one pound per plant.

Indoors under lights, Tanzanian Magic performs well in ebb-and-flow hydro systems and sports a fast-paced cycle. Flowering usually begins after 6 weeks, and finishes in a month to 6 weeks. Finished flowers are more compact than the typical sativa.

Tanzanian Magic provides a burst of energy with its quick onset and electric bite. It is a high with a shorter duration so smokers can moderate how much time of the day to spend recreating with a buzz. This variety is used for medicinal and religious purposes in its homeplace. Its odor summons the harsh slightly unpleasant smokiness of ceremonial incense and the flavor may remind one of hash and bitter medicine—at once acrid, with a cast of phenol and a strong aniseed aftertaste.

African Seeds

Kariba Surprise

Twenty years ago, a group of South African university students began cultivating outdoors as a hobby. For me, alias "Zulu," the hobby became a passion. On holidays or trips within southern Africa, my ambition was to explore remote and beautiful places within Transkei, Swaziland and Lesotho, collecting kind herb and good seed stock.

Over a period of 5-10 years, my friends and I obtained excellent seed stock from the whole region and started looking further north into Zimbabwe, Zambia, Malawi and finally Ethiopia. Our collection was carefully stored and archived for posterity.

The original group of hobby growers began to dissipate in the late 1980s as people moved or went into careers. I, Zulu, continued the collection and the projects that the group had started. In the mid–1990s, I was joined by Jed, a Canadian who spent most of his middle years in Jamaica. The 1990s also saw drug enforcement policies imposed by the U.S. and Europe that introduced spraying programs on a massive scale. Many regional growers and traders were forced to be more covert, and contact was more difficult and less safe.

As breeders, we maintain 3 very strict rules:
1. Only inbreed the very best of each of our collected sativas
2. No cross-breeding sativa stock from various regions
3. Protect biodiversity whenever possible

Already so many famous and mythical African stains have disappeared due to negligence, greed and bad breeding. Several come to mind, such as the legendary hallucinogenic Purple Durban; or the Nigerian Black, with buds so resinous and dark green they appear black. These strains may yet be discovered again.

In 1996, African Seeds was formed. The Internet made it easier to share Africa's special sativa genetics with the world. Recent African Seeds varieties include Ethiopian Highland and Tanzanian Magic, both featured in these pages. We are currently working on some west African strains from Nigeria, Ghana, Senegal and the Gambia as well as some central African sativas, which we hope to release in the future.

Thai-Tanic

Flying Dutchmen

Photo: Green Born Identity

Cannabis aficionados love Thai varieties, but gardeners often find them finicky to grow. Flying Dutchmen's Thai-Tanic crosses a Thai mother with the Original Skunk #1. Skunk #1 is a legendary strain that arrived in Holland from California in the mid-1970s. Many claim it was the first stabilized hybrid in the Netherlands.

Thai-Tanic's hybridization with Skunk is a lasting marriage. First bred by Cultivator's Choice in the early 1980s, this combination has thrived to be a winning match over the years. The Skunk contributes its shorter growing cycle, higher yield and easier maintenance in the garden. Lady Thai lets Skunk rule the grow, but clearly shines through in the final product's clean taste and trippy high.

This variety produces large bracts and medium-sized, resinous buds that resemble big foxtails. The buds keep their weight and structure when dried. The calyx-to-leaf ratio is high. Side branches proliferate but don't stretch out as far as other sativa-dominant strains. This gives Thai-Tanic a balanced, medium profile that reaches one meter (3 feet) of height indoors under a 12/12 light cycle, or up to 3 meters (9 feet) outdoors given a full May–November growing season and no pruning. Indoors, Thai-Tanic's breeders get good results with an arrangement of 9 plants per square meter. In this setup, plants are pruned twice before they flower.

The words "Thai stick" bring a light citrus taste with an edge of tang and a chocolate chaser to the mouths of veteran pot connoisseurs. Thai-Tanic recaptures those sweet-scented memories. The buzz arrives quickly, delivering a vivid trippiness and stoking the mental furnace. Eventually this levels out to dreamy attitude as new concepts drift and play. Thai-Tanic promotes appetite and is reported as an excellent strain for relief of nausea and menstrual cramps.

 85/15

 trippy, dreamy

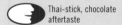 Thai-stick, chocolate aftertaste

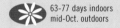 63-77 days indoors mid-Oct. outdoors

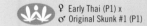 ♀ Early Thai (P1) x ♂ Original Skunk #1 (P1)

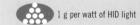 1 g per watt of HID light

 SOG

151

Transskei Green

African Seeds

Transskei Green is the lesser known sister to Durban Poison, named for its region of origin, and for the lime-green coloring of the plants grown in native soil. Wild seeds can be found extensively in the sativa crops acclimated to the Transskei region of South Africa. This area is home to the Wild Coast, known by surfers for its laid back culture, kind waves and even kinder buds.

The native climate has long warm summers, and is mostly semi-arid with sparse arable land, but becomes semi-tropical nearer the coast. African Seeds has inbred this deliciously soulful strain, keeping it pure Wild Coast sativa.

This strain is intended for outdoors, favoring the long grow season of its adapted region. It is a tall plant, averaging between 9 and 12 feet in height. The long slender "Lambs Bread" type buds reach lengths of 2 feet or longer. Under optimal conditions, Transskei Green yields 20-30 ounces of dried manicured bud from a single plant in a 10-14 week flowering cycle.

The Transskei Green high is like a cool refreshing breeze blowing through one's thoughts. The flavors begin with an earthy taste like strong coffee and ends with aniseed, the flavoring in licorice. The sensation is clear and energetic, resembling the effects that African genetics are famous for. This variety can be enjoyed while still maintaining focus for work or creative endeavors. In Transskei, it is used as an herbal medicine for ailments ranging from asthma to impotence.

 clear, energetic

 licorice, coffee

 70-100 days

 Transskei sativa

 600-750 g (20-25 oz.) per plant

Waldo: A Tribute

Waldo was named for John "Waldo" Cliver, a medical cannabis user and activist who died in 2004 at the age of 39. Waldo suffered from spina bifida, a debilitating birth defect to the neural tube. In his case, his mind was fully intact, but his spinal cord was cleft and partly exposed, restricting him to a wheelchair. His body also suffered other complications that made eating a project, and pain management essential.

Despite the difficulties of his condition, Waldo had an active life and lots of ideas. In the late 1980s, Waldo began cultivating and smoking marijuana. It was good medicine for his mind and for his medical condition. His garden was even written up in *High Times* in a July 2000 feature by his longtime friend Kyle Kushman. After the article, Waldo became more involved in the cannabis scene, attending events like the NORML convention in San Francisco, and the Cannabis Cup in Amsterdam. He made friends among other cannabis compatriots.

Photo: Linda Senti, Eddy's Medicinal Gardens

Then, in March 2003, police raided his grow. New Jersey had no protections for medical users, so a court battle began. It overshadowed the last 7 months of his life. Known for his stubbornness, Waldo was determined to make no deals, and began his legal battle.

Just before his arrest, Waldo visited the gardens of Eddy and Linda Lepp in northern California. The Lepp's run a Cannabis Ministry , which serves as a center for the medical marijuana community. The support network was unlike anything Waldo had ever experienced. He moved to the ministry, and it was at this sanctuary where he lived the last months of his life. Apothecary breeders came to know Waldo through the Lepp's. They say "Waldo had spirit and a hell of a laugh. His family said he'd never been happier than he was during this time of his life. Waldo is greatly missed by all who knew him. I named the strain after him because he was a fallen brother."

Photo: Bobby B.

Waldo

Apothecary

75/25

cerebral, long lasting

spicy

58-65 days indoors
late Sept. – beg. Oct.
outdoors

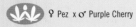♀ Pez x ♂ Purple Cherry

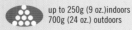up to 250g (9 oz.)indoors
700g (24 oz.) outdoors

SOG

Waldo got its name, not from the elusive character of children's books, but as a tribute to a medical pot patient activist and friend of the Apothecary breeders. The Waldo strain is well adapted to cool climates, growing with incredible vigor even in the Netherlands.

A patch of this 7-foot cannabis might look more like a Christmas tree farm than a pot grove. Outdoor finishing time is fast—buds are ready for harvest by early Autumn. In more conducive latitudes, Waldo can reach monster sizes. Plants that were started early and vegetated indoors reportedly grew to multi-meter heights and breadths, and yielded nearly 2000 grams per plant.

The indoor-cultivated Waldo is a scaled down version of its outdoor sibling, reaching an average height of about one meter (3 feet). These little sisters still spread their stout branches wide and average 2-4 feet in diameter—almost as wide or wider than their height. These plump gals will have to be trimmed to fit their ideal size and space of one plant per square foot. Apothecary recommends organic fertilizers regardless of growing method, with the understanding that the fewer synthetic chemicals fed to a medicinal plant, the better.

Clean, organic growing also contributes to a cooler, smoother smoke and a distinct aroma from dried buds. Waldo burns spicy and pungent, maybe a little musty, like a warm, spicy red wine. The high is a thought-expander, like sativa, but with some body stoniness and durability from its indica heritage. This is the kind of balanced experience sought by social smokers as well as connoisseurs looking for a new mainstay smoke that will continue to deliver over time.

Warlock

Magus Genetics

"Warlock" connotes a master of the dark arts, a male witch or magus. Magus Genetics' Warlock strain comes from a wizard's pouch of indica-dominant bag seed. Magus estimates that, for the current generation of Warlock, the male was inbred for two generations longer than the pre-2000 Warlock, then crossed back to the original Warlock mother. The pot that springs up from these seeds offers good indoor growing traits and a thinker's high.

Appropriately enough, this variety finishes flowering around Halloween, so it belongs indoors in climates with a gloomy autumn. Given good indoor light, the plant grows outward almost as much as it grows upward, filling the available space. Growers may have to be ruthless in their pruning of branches or the removal of plants to avoid crowding and maximize the light to the buds, and therefore the yield per square meter. Although Warlock likes to branch, it is not very leafy—those that do show up are medium-sized and easy to manicure. With proper attention to space, Warlock can be grown in any style or any of the usual mediums.

With a raisin-like palate verging on sour candy and a stimulating buzz, this strain is a good choice to replace sweet tobacco as the companion to coffee. A Warlock joint paired with plenty of good java can aid focus, dry up sodden thoughts, and may help relieve attention problems like attention deficit/hyperactive disorder and depression. Warlock won third place in the 1997 *High Times* Cannabis Cup (bio category) when entered by the Bluebird coffeeshop.

stimulating

sweet & sour

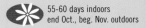
55-60 days indoors
end Oct., beg. Nov. outdoors

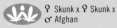
♀ Skunk x ♀ Skunk x
♂ Afghan

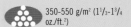
350-550 g/m² (1¹/₃-1³/₄
oz./ft.²)

SOG

155

White Light

Soma Seeds

 60/40

 creeper, sensual, relaxing

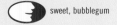 sweet, bubblegum

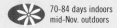 70-84 days indoors
mid-Nov. outdoors

 ♀ White Widow x
♂ Bubblegum

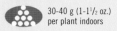 30-40 g (1-1½ oz.)
per plant indoors

 SOG

156

White Light is a cannabis thoroughbred derived from two popular, multiple award-winning strains, the tasty Bubble Gum and the potent White Widow. Bubble Gum dates back to the 1970s pot underground in the United States while the younger White Widow became a Dutch coffeehouse staple in the 1990s. White Light is a trans-Atlantic marriage made in Amsterdam.

Bubble Gum strains grow in two phenotypes: one is the traditional "Christmas-tree" shape. The other is a vertical "pole" pattern with few branches and large top colas. Bubble Gum's daughter White Light is all pole – thus very suitable for sea of green planting. Her big top growth sports hard, compact buds. The plant rises to 3 feet indoors. When grown outdoors in the tropical climate she loves, she can reach a gargantuan 12 feet.

If necessary, height can be controlled by clipping and keeping the vegetative phase to a minimum by flower forcing early. White Light's leaves and buds have inherited the copious resin production of her White Widow father. For the overeager, finger hash can be made by rubbing the sweet, clear THC crystals off the plant after her sixth week of flowering.

Soma selects plants for their potential medicinal value as well as pleasure. White Light is nerve balm with good potential as a painkiller. However, the pleasure aspect is far from forgotten. It begins with the tasty sweet smoke, and builds slowly as a strong end-of-the-day relaxer high. Speaking of pleasure, this variety is rumored to have a touch of aphrodisiac in the mix. "Great for getting in bed with a loved one," Soma adds. "Do not use this weed for going to court." Here's to less time spent arguing and more time spent snuggling!

White Star

Delta-9 Labs

White Star gets its name for its trichome-coated limbs that point out like rays in every direction. This strain is the sativa-dominant progeny of two highly awarded strains: Paradise Seed's Sensi Star, winner of High Life and *High Times* awards in 1999 and 2000; and Soma's New York City Diesel, three-time Cannabis Cup winner and a favorite among the Amsterdam crowd. Conventional wisdom says that sativas give smokers a "head high" in contrast to the indica "body high." White Star successfully mixes the two for a buzz that both tingles the pores and opens the third eye.

Recommended for indoor gardens, this variety's flowers may begin to reach maturity at around 9 weeks but the average time is closer to 10 weeks. At this point or a little earlier, the calyxes start to bulge. Some gardeners prolong the bloom to between 10 and 12 weeks for continued trichome production. White Star forms many individual main stem branches that grow very tall and sprout long thick leaves. The internodes or branching points seem unusually far apart at first, but they fill in fast as the growing cycle progresses. This plant produces the best yields when multiple branches are selected and kept.

This sweet tasting variety delivers an uplifting mixture of mind and body buzz that can be energizing and profoundly psychedelic. The celebrity match contributes stellar qualities to the high; however, the Diesel parentage creates a sense of brain acceleration and the Sensi Star makes the high come on fast and strong, so some pacing may be advisable. As long as it isn't overdone, the result should be a giddy animation, which could be harnessed to complete projects around the house or to enjoy with friends for a night out on the town.

 80/20

 uplifting

 sweet

 75-80 days

 ♀ NYC Diesel x ♂ Sensi Star

 400-550g/m² (1¹/₂-1³/₄ oz./ft.²)

Afghanica • Ambrosia • Aurora Indica • Australian Blue • Biddy Early • Blue
Brains Escape • Bronze Whaler • California Grapefruit • Candy Cane Brain •
Diamond Head • Double Dutch • Dreadlock • Ducksfoot • Dutch Treat x North
Euforia • Exile • G13-Haze x NYC Diesel • God's Treat • Hawaiian Snow • He
Kerala Krush • Lethal Purple • Lionheart • Lowryder • Magic Bud • Manitoba
Ultra • Moroc x Afgan • New York City Diesel • Nirvana Special • Orange Bud
Treat • Rocklock • RockStar • Rox • Sage 'n Sour • Sapphire Star • Sativa Spi
• Sour Diesel • StarGazer • Strawberry Cough • Sugar Babe • Super Shit • Sv
Light • White Star • Afghanica • Ambrosia • Aurora Indica • Australian Blue •
• Brains Damage • Brains Escape • Bronze Whaler • California Grapefruit • Ca
• Danky Doodle • Diamond Head • Double Dutch • Dreadlock • Ducksfoot •
Ethiopian Highland • Euforia • Exile • G13-Haze x NYC Diesel • God's Treat •
#39 • KC #42 • Kerala Krush • Lethal Purple • Lionheart • Lowryder • Magic B
• Mikush • MK-Ultra • Moroc x Afgan • New York City Diesel • Nirvana Specia
Skunk x Dutch Treat • Rocklock • RockStar • Rox • Sage 'n Sour • Sapphire St
Amnesia Haze • Sour Diesel • StarGazer • Strawberry Cough • Sugar Babe •
Warlock • White Light • White Star • Afghanica • Ambrosia • Aurora Indica • Au
• Brains Choice • Brains Damage • Brains Escape • Bronze Whaler • California
• Cinderella 99 • Danky Doodle • Diamond Head • Double Dutch • Dreadlock
Endless Sky • Ethiopian Highland • Euforia • Exile • G13-Haze x NYC Diesel •
Surprise • KC #39 • KC #42 • Kerala Krush • Lethal Purple • Lionheart • Lowry
Mint • Mazar • Mikush • MK-Ultra • Moroc x Afgan • New York City Diesel • N
Plant • Purple Skunk x Dutch Treat • Rocklock • RockStar • Rox • Sage 'n Sou
White • Soma's Amnesia Haze • Sour Diesel • StarGazer • Strawberry Cough
Green • Waldo • Warlock • White Light • White Star • Afghanica • Ambrosia • A
• Bluberry Haze • Brains Choice • Brains Damage • Brains Escape • Bronze W
Cherry Pez Livity • Cinderella 99 • Danky Doodle • Diamond Head • Double

Appendixes

Company Acknowledgments

African Seeds
Ethiopian Highland
Kariba Surprise
Tanzanian Magic
Transkei Green

www.africanseeds.com
seeds@africanseeds.com

Almighty Seeds
Lionheart

27 Lapsley Road, Suite 25
Scarborough, ON   M1B 1K1
Canada
www.almightyseeds.com
www.seedbank.com

Apothecary
Cherry Pez Livity
Waldo

www.apothecaryseeds.com
apothecaryseeds420@hotmail.com
tel: +31 (0)65 084-1982

Bonguru Beans
RockStar
Shiesel

bongurubeans@hotmail.com

Delta-9 Labs
CannaSutra
StarGazer
White Star

Bentinckstraat 7
1051 GC Amsterdam
The Netherlands
www.delta9labs.com
info@delta9labs.com
tel: +31 (0)62 658-2966

DNA Genetics
Bluberry Haze
California Grapefruit
Cannalope Haze
Rocklock

www.dnagenetics.ca
info@dnagenetics.ca
fax: +31 (0)20 771-8366

Dutch Passion
Euforia
Mazar
Orange Bud
Power Plant
Strawberry Cough

Seeds of Passion Amsterdam
Utrechsestr. 26
1017 VN Amsterdam
The Netherlands

tel: +31 (0)20 625-1100

Seeds of Passion Maastricht
Grote Gracht 40
6211 SX Maastricht
The Netherlands
tel: +31 (0)43 321-5848
www.seedsofpassion.nl
www.dutch-passion.nl

East Island Seed Company
Dutch Treat x Northern Lights
Purple Skunk x Dutch Treat

Represented by:
The Great Canadian Seed Company
PO Box 29026
1950 West Broadway
Vancouver, B.C. V6J 5C2
Canada
www.greatcanadianseeds.com
info@greatcanadianseeds.com
tel: (604) 528-0336

Electric Seed Company
Blue Grape #1

Represented by:
Seed Bank of Canada
PO Box 174
2416 Main Street
Vancouver, B.C. V5T 3E2
Canada
www.theseedbankofcanada.com
tel: (604) 251-6316

Federation Seed Company
Mikush

Represented by:
The Amsterdam Seed Company of
Canada
PO Box 4253
349 West Georgia Street
Vancouver, B.C. V6B 3Z7
Canada
www.theamsterdam.com
sales@theamsterdam.com
info@theamsterdam.com
tel: (604) 763-5617

Flying Dutchmen
Afghanica
Kerala Krush
Pineapple Punch
Thai-Tanic

Mail: PO Box 10952
1001 EZ Amsterdam
The Netherlands

Shop: O.Z. Achterburgwal 131
1012 DE Amsterdam
The Netherlands
www.flyingdutchmen.com
admin@flyingdutchmen.com

Great White North

Early Sativa
Lethal Purple
Manitoba Poison

Represented by:
AAA Seed Company
PO Box 72088
Sasamat RPO
Vancouver, B.C. V6R 4P2
Canada
www.aaa-weedseed.com
info@aaa-weedseed.com
tel: (604) 880-2829

Greenhouse Seed Company

Hawaiian Snow

Mail: PO Box 75162
1070 AD Amsterdam
The Netherlands

Shop: O.Z. Voorburgwal 191
1012 EW Amsterdam
The Netherlands

www.greenhouse.org
info@greenhouse.org
tel: +31 (0)20 427-3059
fax: +31 (0)20 427-3059

Greenthumb Seeds

Early Swazi Skunk
Endless Sky

PO Box 37085
Ottawa, ON K0C 1T0
Canada
www.drgreenthumb.com
mail@drgreenthumb.com
info line: (613) 527-3090

Gypsy Nirvana

Cinderella 99

Mail: Gypsy Nirvana's Seed Boutique
PO Box 10578
1001 EN Amsterdam
The Netherlands

Shop: Gypsy Nirvana's Seed Boutique
163 Singel
1001 EN Amsterdam
The Netherlands

In England:
Gypsy Nirvana/Seeds Direct
55 Surbiton Road
Kingston-upon-Thames
Surrey KT1 2HT
England

www.seedboutique.com
www.seedsdirect.to
www.seedbay.com

info@seedboutique.com
gypsynirvana@hotmail.com
info@seedsdirect.to

Homegrown Fantaseeds
Australian Blue
Blue Pearl
Shiva

Mail: H.F.
PO Box 3204
1001 AA Amsterdam
The Netherlands

Shop: Fantaseeds Garden
Nieuwe Nieuwstraat 25
1012 NG Amsterdam
The Netherlands

www.homegrown-fantaseeds.com
mail@homegrown-fantaseeds.com

Joint Doctor's High-Bred Seeds
Dreadlock
Lowryder

High Bred
PO Box 70802
C.P. Chabanel
Montreal, QC H2N 2L2
Canada
www.highbred.net

Jordan of the Islands
Ambrosia
Blue God
God's Treat
Sapphire Star

Represented by:
AAA Seed Company
PO Box 72088
Sasamat RPO
Vancouver, B.C. V6R 4P2
Canada
www.aaa-weedseed.com
info@aaa-weedseed.com
tel: (604) 880-2829

KC Brains
Brains Choice
Brains Damage
Brains Escape
Danky Doodle
KC #39
KC #42

PO Box 637
4200 AP Gorinchem
The Netherlands
www.kcbrains.com
tel: +31 (0)65 473-0608
fax: +31 (0)18 363-6510

Magus Genetics
Biddy Early
Double Dutch
Exile
Warlock

Mail: PO Box 36
1600 AA Enkhuizen
The Netherlands

Shop: Vijzelstraat 52
1601 NK Enkhuizen
The Netherlands

www.magusgenetics.com
magus@hetnet.nl
tel: +31 (0)22 832-3441
fax: +31 (0)22 832-3467

Mandala Seeds
Kalichakra
Satori

www.mandalaseeds.com
mandalaseeds@hotmail.com
fax: +49 (0)89 24 433-6403

MJOZ
Bronze Whaler

MG Club
PO Box 43
Lake Heights NSW 2502
Australia

http://mjoz.nexodus.tv
info@mjoz.nexodus.tv

Nirvana
Aurora Indica
Moroc x Afgan
Nirvana Special
Papaya
Snow White

Mail: PO Box 51071
1007 EA Amsterdam
The Netherlands

Shop: Toldwarsstraat 24 Winkel
1073 RR Amsterdam
The Netherlands

www.nirvana.nl
info@nirvana.nl
tel: +31 (0)20 364-0233
fax: +31 (0)20 671-3745

Paradise Seeds
Magic Bud
Rox
Sativa Spirit
Sugar Babe
Swiss Bliss

PO Box 377
1000 AJ Amsterdam
The Netherlands

www.paradise-seeds.com
info@paradise-seeds.com
tel: +31 (0)20 679-5422
fax: +31 (0)20 679-5422

Reservoir Seeds
Sour Diesel

Represented by:
Gypsy Nirvana/Seeds Direct
55 Surbiton Road
Kingston-upon-Thames
Surrey KT1 2HT
England

Gypsy Nirvana's Seed Boutique
163 Singel
1001 EN Amsterdam
The Netherlands

www.seedsdirect.to
www.seedboutique.com
gypsynirvana@hotmail.com

Sagarmatha Seeds
Diamond Head
Matanuska Mint
Slyder

Mail: PO Box 3717
1001 AM Amsterdam
The Netherlands

Shop: St. Nicolaasstraat 38
1012 NK Amsterdam
The Netherlands

www.highestseeds.com
www.sagarmatha.nl
info@highestseeds.com
tel: +31 (0)20 638-4334
fax: +31 (0)20 420-9875

Seedbank.com
Passion Queen
Super Shit

www.seedbank.com
seedbankdotcom@canada.com

Sensi Seed Bank
Jack Flash
Maple Leaf Indica
Marley's Collie

Mail: PO Box 1771
3000 BT Rotterdam
The Netherlands

Shop: Oudezijds Achterburgwal 150
1012 DV Amsterdam
The Netherlands

www.sensiseeds.com
info@sensiseeds.com
tel: +31 (0)20 624-0386
fax: +31 (0)20 624-2433

Shadow Seed Company
Candy Cane Brain

Represented by:
Seed Bank of Canada
PO Box 174
2416 Main Street
Vancouver, B.C. V5T 3E2
Canada
www.theseedbankofcanada.com
tel: (604) 251-6316

Soma Seeds
G-13 Haze x NYC Diesel
New York City Diesel
Soma's Amnesia Haze
White Light

PO Box 16491
1001 RN Amsterdam
The Netherlands
www.somaseeds.nl
soma@somaseeds.nl
tel: +31 (0)65 474-5083

T.H. Seeds
Heavy Duty Fruity
MK-Ultra
Sage 'n Sour

Nieuwendijk 13
1012 LZ Amsterdam
The Netherlands

www.thseeds.com
info@thseeds.com
tel: +31 (0)20 421-1762
fax: +31 (0)20 421-0991

Wally Duck
Ducksfoot

Represented by:
Gypsy Nirvana/ Seeds Direct
55 Surbiton Road
Kingston-upon-Thames
Surrey KT1 2HT
England
www.seedsdirect.to
wallyduck@hotmail.com

Willy Jack
Skydog

WJSC
609 Dundas Street
Suite 2
London, ON N5W 2Z1
Canada
willyjack@canada.com
tel: (866) 368-4250

Glossary

apical tip– the growing tip of the plant

backcrossing– crossing of an offspring with one of the parents to reinforce a trait

bract– small reduced leaflet in cannabis that appears below a pair of calyxes

calyx– pod harboring the female ovule and two pistils; seed pod

F1 generation– first filial generation, the offspring of two parent (P-1) plants

F2 generation– second filial generation, the offspring of two f-1 plants

hydroponics– growing plants in nutrient solution without soil

indica– plant originating in the 30th parallel typified by wide, dark green leaves sometimes bordering on purple. Short internodes and profuse branching form a wide pyramid shape usually no more than 3 1/2 feet tall

internodes– the space between nodes

node– a section of the stem where leaves and side shoots arise. Nodes are often swollen, and are sometimes referred to as joints

P1– first parental generation, the parents crossed to form F1 or F1 hybrid offspring

petiole– the stem of the leaf. It attaches to the plant stem

pistils– small pair of fuzzy white hairs extending from top of calyx, the flower's female organ

pollen– the male reproductive product that fertilizes the female flower. It is a cream-colored or yellow dust released by the male flower, and floats along air currents to reach the female

sativa– plant originating from the 45-50th parallel typified by a tall pine-tree-like growth habit(5 to 15 feet), long internodes, light green color and airy buds

sea of green (SOG)– indoor method for growing marijuana. Many plants are grown close together with little time spent in vegetative growth. Rather than a few plants growing large and filling the canopy, many smaller plants are forced into flowering creating a lower canopy and earlier harvest

sepal– a modified leaf located at the base of a flower

stigma– the two "hairs" sticking up from each marijuana flower. When young, they are white or cream-colored, although they sometimes have purple tints. They mine the air for pollen. When pollinated or stale, they dry and turn tan, red or purple

stipule– the section where the plant stem meets the leaf stem, or petiole

strain– a line of offspring derived from common ancestors

THC– tetrahydrocannabinol, primary psychoactive component of cannabis

trichome– plant hair that is either glandular (secreting) or eglandular (non secreting) in function

When Will Your Outdoor Plants Mature?

Cannabis flowers based on the number of hours of uninterrupted dark period it receives. When a critical period is reached for several days the plant changes its growth from vegetative to flowering. During the spring and summer the number of hours of darkness shrinks as the latitude increases. For instance, on June 16, close to June 22, the longest day of the year and the first day of summer, there are 9:30 hours of darkness at the 35th latitude, near Memphis, Albuquerque and Los Angeles. At the 40th parallel, close to New York, Columbus and Denver the dark period is 9 hours. A difference of half an hour. However, the seed producer's latitudes are considerably different

Amsterdam Flame strain outdoors Photo credit: Paradise Seeds

than the latitudes of the gardens of many outdoor growers. Vancouver, at the 50th parallel and Holland at the 52nd parallel have 7:49 and 7:27 of darkness respectively on that date. As a result maturity dates change significantly with changes in latitude.

To find the ripening date at your latitude:

1.) Count back from the outdoor ripening date the number of days the variety takes to flower indoors. This is the trigger date, the date that the plant changes from vegetative to flowering phase.

2.) Locate the breeder's latitude at the trigger date. The chart (next page) indicates the number of hours of darkness that triggered the plant to flower.

3.) On the column representing your latitude, locate the date on the chart that matches the dark period from #2.

4.) Count forward the number of days it takes to ripen indoors. The result is the maturity date.

Figuring Ripening Dates: Examples

A variety from Holland ripens there on October 15 and matures in 70 days indoors. Counting back on the latitude chart you see that on August 1, about 75 days before ripening, the plant triggered on 8½ hours of darkness. Along the 40th parallel or further south, the dark period never gets below 9 hours of darkness. The variety will be triggered to flower almost as soon as it is placed outside. If it's planted outdoors June 1 it will ripen in 70 days, near August 10. If planted June 16 it will ripen in late August. At the 45th parallel, the plant will be triggered to flower around July 1. The buds will mature September 10-15.

A Canadian variety adapted to the 50th parallel ripens October 16 outdoors, 60 days after forcing indoors. Counting back to Aug 16, 60 days before the bud matures, the dark period at the 50th parallel is about 9½ hours. At the 45th parallel this dark period occurs August 4, with a ripening date of around October 4. At the 40th parallel it occurs around July 30, with a harvest around September 30. At the 35th parallel and lower latitudes, flowering is triggered as soon as the plants are planted since there are only a few days around June 22 when the dark period stretches longer than 9½ hours. If planted June 1, the plants will ripen in early August.

NUMBER OF HOURS OF DARKNESS BY LATITUDE

Latitude	0	+10	+20	+30	+35	+40	+45	+50	+52	+54	+56	+58
June 16	11:53	11:18	10:40	9:56	9:30	8:59	8:24	7:49	7:27	6:53	6:25	5:53
July 1	11:53	11:18	10:41	9:57	9:31	9:01	8:26	7:41	7:21	6:57	6:29	5:55
July 16	11:53	11:21	10:46	10:08	9:44	9:17	8:45	8:05	7:47	7:25	7:01	7:33
Aug. 1	11:53	11:27	10:59	10:26	10:06	9:44	9:19	8:48	8:32	8:15	7:57	7:35
Aug. 16	11:53	11:34	11:13	10:48	10:33	10:17	9:58	9:35	9:27	9:12	9:59	9:43
Sept. 1	11:53	11:42	11:29	11:15	11:06	10:57	10:45	10:29	10.25	10:18	10:10	10:02
Sept. 16	11:53	11:50	11:46	11:41	11:39	11:35	11:31	11:27	11:24	11:22	11:21	11:16
Oct. 1	11:53	11:59	12:03	12:08	12:11	12:14	12:18	12:22	12:24	12:26	12:28	12:30
Oct. 16	11:53	12:07	12:19	12:35	12:43	12:53	13:06	13:17	13:23	13:30	13:36	13:45
Nov. 1	11:53	12:13	12:36	13:01	13:15	13:31	13:49	14:14	14:24	14:35	14:48	15:03
Nov. 16	11:53	12:21	12:50	13:22	13:42	14:03	14:29	15:00	15:14	15:30	15:49	16:09
Dec. 1	11:53	12:26	13:00	13:39	14:03	14:27	14:58	15:36	16:07	16:14	16:36	17:02
Dec. 16	11:53	12:27	13:05	13:56	14:12	14:40	15:12	15:54	16:13	16:36	17:01	17:31

Seed Producers Latitude Chart:

Australia, Nimbin: Latitude 30° S

Canada: Ottawa–Toronto, Ontario: Latitude 43° N
        Vancouver (incl. Nanaimo), British Columbia: Latitude 50° N

Holland: Latitude 52° N

Malawi: Latitudes 10–15° S

Spain: Latitude 39–41° N

Swaziland: Latitude 26° S

Switzerland: Latitude: 47° N

METRIC CONVERSION

Mass

1 gram = .035 ounces (1/3 ounce)

1 ounce = 28.35 grams

1 pound = 16 ounces

1 kilogram = 2.2 pounds

1 pound = .45 kilograms (about 1/2 kilogram)

Length

1 foot = 30.5 centimeters (1/3 meter)

1 meter = 3.28 feet

1 meter = 100 centimeters

1 inch = 2.54 centimeters

Area

1 square meter = 10.76 square feet

1 square foot = .09 square meters (about 1/10 meter)

Yield

1 ounce per square foot = 305 g per square meter

100 grams per square meter = 3.25 ounces per square foot

Temperature

15°C = 59°F

20°C = 68°F

25°C = 72°F

28°C = 82°F

30°c = 86°F

32°C = 89.5°F

35°C = 95° F

To figure:

Celsius = (F - 32) * 5/9

Fahrenheit = C * 9/5 + 32

Index

Lowryder
Magic Bud
RockStar
Rox
Sativa Spirit
Satori
Shiva
Sugar Babe
Super Shit
Warlock

 Sativa Dominant Strains (60% to 90%)
Blue Pearl
Euforia
G-13 Haze x NYC Diesel
Kerala Krush
Nirvana Special
Orange Bud
Pineapple Punch
Power Plant
Sage 'n Sour
Soma's Amnesia Haze
Strawberry Cough
Swiss Bliss
Thai-Tanic
White Star

 Sativa Strains (90% to 100%)
Australian Blue
Cannalope Haze
Early Sativa
Early Swazi Skunk

Ethiopian Highland
Hawaiian Snow
Kariba Surprise
KC #42
Lionheart
Sour Diesel
Tanzanian Magic
Transkei Green

Varieties by Environment

Note that the category may be in part determined by the area of origin. Strains indicated for outdoor gardening (including indoor/outdoor strains) may only be recommended as such for certain regions. See the variety's description for more detailed information.

 Indoor Strains
Aurora Indica
Australian Blue
Bronze Whaler
Double Dutch
Exile
G-13 Haze x NYC Diesel
Hawaiian Snow
Jack Flash
KC #42
MK-Ultra
Moroc x Afgan
Nirvana Special
Papaya
Purple Skunk x Dutch Treat
Rocklock

Sage 'n Sour
Shiesel
Shiva
Slyder
Snow White
Sour Diesel
StarGazer
Strawberry Cough
White Star

 Outdoor Strains
Ducksfoot
Early Sativa
Early Swazi Skunk
Kariba Surprise
Lethal Purple
Lionheart
Manitoba Poison
Transkei Green

 Indoor/Outdoor Strains
Afghanica
Ambrosia
Biddy Early
Bluberry Haze
Blue God
Blue Grape #1
Blue Pearl
Brains Choice
Brains Damage
Brains Escape
California Grapefruit
Candy Cane Brain

Cannalope Haze
CannaSutra
Cherry Pez Livity
Cinderella 99
Danky Doodle
Diamond Head
Dreadlock
Dutch Treat x Northern Lights
Endless Sky
Ethiopian Highland
Euforia
God's Treat
Heavy Duty Fruity
Kalichakra
KC #39
Kerala Krush
Lowryder
Magic Bud
Maple Leaf Indica
Marley's Collie
Matanuska Mint
Mazar
Mikush
New York City Diesel
Orange Bud
Passion Queen
Pineapple Punch
Power Plant
RockStar
Rox
Sapphire Star
Sativa Spirit
Satori

Skydog
Soma's Amnesia Haze
Sugar Babe
Super Shit
Swiss Bliss
Tanzanian Magic
Thai-Tanic
Waldo
Warlock
White Light

Greenhouse Recommended Varieties

While many all-around strains can perform well in the greenhouse, the following were particularly noted by breeders as appropriate for greenhouse cultivation.

Biddy Early
Brains Damage
Brains Escape
Kerala Krush
Marley's Collie
Matanuska Mint
Mazar
Power Plant
Passion Queen
Sativa Spirit
Skydog
Soma's Amnesia Haze
Strawberry Cough
Sugar Babe
Swiss Bliss
Waldo

Sea of Green Recommended Varieties

Afghanica
Ambrosia
Aurora Indica
Blue Pearl
Brains Damage
Bronze Whaler
California Grapefruit
Candy Cane Brain
Cannalope Haze
Cherry Pez Livity
Diamond Head
Dreadlock
Dutch Treat x Northern Lights
Endless Sky
Euforia
Exile
Heavy Duty Fruity
Jack Flash
Lowryder
Magic Bud
Manitoba Poison
Maple Leaf Indica
Marley's Collie
Mazar
MK-Ultra
Moroc x Afgan
Orange Bud
Papaya
Passion Queen
Pineapple Punch
Power Plant

Essays & Stories

The Big Book of **BUDS**

thanks the businesses that supported this project.

www.bigbookofbuds.com

Online photo gallery of the best majijuana in the world.

179

180

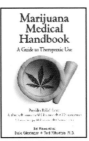

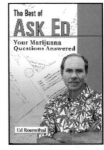

Ahh. . .Full melt. . .

The stuff of connoisseurs. Bubble Bags are the world's only filtration system that offers up to seven layers of filtering, which ensures that you get the highest quality yield. For more information, please visit our website or call (866)-MELTING (635-8464).

Fresh Headies presents

BUBBLE BAGS

http://www.bubblebag.com

Santa Cruz

Compassion Flower Inn

A bed, bud and breakfast serving the medical marijuana community and all world travelers who honor the many uses of the hemp plant.

216 Laurel Street, Santa Cruz, California 95060 / phone 831 466-0420

187

CANNABIS SATIVA L

188

Quick Key to Icons

Strain Type

Sativa

Indica

Sativa/Indica

Indica/Sativa

Growing Info

Flowering time
Tiempo de floración
Blütezeit
Durée de floraison
Stagione della fioritura
Bloetijd

Parents
Genética
Mutterpflanze
Descendance
Genitori
Stamboom

Yield
Rendimiento
Ertag
Rendement
Raccolta
Opbrengst

Indoor
Interior
Drinnen
d´Intérieur
Dentro
Binnen

Outdoor
Exterior
Draussen
d´Extérieur
Fuori
Buiten

Indoor/Outdoor
Interior/Exterior
Drinnen/Draussen
d´Intérieur/d´Extérieur
Dentro/Fuori
Binnen/Buiten

SOG
Sea of Green

Sensory Experience

Buzz
Efecto
die Art des Turns
Effets
Effetti
High Effekt

Taste/Smell
Sabor/Aroma
Geschmack/Geruch
Saveur/Arôme
Sapore/Odore
Smaak/Geua

Breeder Location

South Africa

Australia

Canada

Netherlands

Spain